Lady and Jesse Make a Promise

Love, Faith, Lost and Found

Larry B. Bachman

Music and Video Credits:
Words and music by Larry B. Bachman
Music video produced by Larry B. Bachman

Players:
Vocals—lead and backup: Shana Saint
Guitars—acoustic and electric: Scott Bachman
Guitars, piano, electronics: Arron Delosantos
Percussion: Erick Morgan

Video director: Nancy Criss
Video post-production engineer: James LaViola
Music engineer, mix-down, and mastering: Patrick McGuire
Photography and video: Javid and Liz Johnson
Co-producers: Nancy Criss and Kenneth Hampton

World rights reserved. This book or any portion thereof may not be copied or reproduced in any form or manner whatever, except as provided by law, without the written permission of the publisher, except by a reviewer who may quote brief passages in a review.

The author assumes full responsibility for the accuracy of all facts and quotations as cited in this book. The opinions expressed in this book are the author's personal views and interpretations, and do not necessarily reflect those of the publisher.

This book is provided with the understanding that the publisher is not engaged in giving spiritual, legal, medical, or other professional advice. If authoritative advice is needed, the reader should seek the counsel of a competent professional.

Copyright © 2024 Larry B. Bachman
Copyright © 2024 TEACH Services, Inc.
ISBN-13: 978-1-4796-1659-6 (Paperback)
ISBN-13: 978-1-4796-1660-2 (ePub)
Library of Congress Control Number: 2023915823

All scripture quotations are taken from the King James Version. Public domain.

TABLE OF CONTENTS

Foreword   v

Preface   vii

Future Tense   9

Starting at the Beginning   13

A Time Ago   15

Jesse Defined   19

A Bible-verse Shootout, a Baptism, and a Fair   23

Lady Makes a Statement   37

The Ballad of Lady and Jesse In Tune   47

Home at the Parsons   59

Back to the Future and Then Some   83

Success at a Cost   85

Can We Ever Go Home Again?   99

Almost Home   111

Drama and Grief   123

The Inheritance   131

Affirmation and Discovery   143

"Discovery of Truth" Concert   155

Afterword   161

Lyrics: "The Gift"   163

Lyrics: "I Will See You"   164

Music Score: "The Promise"   165

In Memory of Scott Bachman   177

Poem: "An Old Man's Lament"   179

FOREWORD

Lady and Jesse Make a Promise exemplifies the extraordinary works of Larry B. Bachman. Each captivating page presents ideas that are beautifully expressed. This fictitious presentation depicts a real-life story of two individuals who are determined to fulfill a sincere promise that inspired the magnificent production of *The Promise*, a musical representation of that commitment.

Bachman captures the beauty of an almost-lost talent. His style of writing is refreshing; the imagery makes you feel as if you are planted in the very midst of the scenes. Keeping the attention of readers is an important aspect of writing, and Bachman does. The way in which the tone, words, and mood of each event fit together perfectly leaves very little room for boredom and showcases his skill as a writer.

Skillful authors are often sought after and sometimes hard to find, but there is no reason for you to look any further. Bachman has published several books that attest to his remarkable talent, but this piece in particular has impacted my life in a very special way; it reminds me of the fact that life is short, and time should be used wisely. Additionally, it entices you to examine and experience life's challenges by connecting you to the source of solutions rather than focusing on problems. I invite you to invest in a worthwhile production!

—Estrella Delgadillo, RN, ND

P. S. This book is a lively, fictional literary rendering based on true events.

PREFACE

Responding to the call for quietude and the challenge of homesteading, our family moved to the country. I believed that this would afford me more time to write and tend to some of the manuscripts that were awaiting completion. Much to my wondering surprise—are you kidding me—oh, the chores, the prep time for the garden, clearing brush and trees, removing fence, and the endless bush hogging. There are animals that need tending, too. You must be on constant lookout for predators who like eggs and the chickens that produce them. You have to build runs with fences that protect top, bottom, sides, and underneath, yet allow free range during the day. Then you make sure they are back to safety and accounted for by nightfall. Yes, there's a lot more to homesteading and the *Green Acres* image than I had imagined at the outset.

What's this got to do with the book, you might ask? Plainly, I have come full circle. I grew up on a farm. So did Lady, the main character of this story. I left that safety and quietude of farm life and shuffled off to try to find my pot of gold at the end of the musical rainbow. So did Lady. Lady grew up with good, loving, faith-based parents, and so did I. She lost her way many times in her story … so did I. Lady thought that she could not be forgiven for what she had done … and yes, so did I.

For a parental point of view, I will use the analogy of the chicken run. As parents, we build a safety net to surround our babies. We care for our children, nurture them, and provide a balance of love, kindness, and instruction to protect them from whatever pitfalls might affect their growth. As a parent you may choose to include faith-based, Biblical instruction into their curriculum, which I highly recommend.

Then, too soon there comes the time when we open the gate, and it is out into the free range they go. Prayer for travel mercy to school, shopping, church, a friend's, and then home again. We breathe a sigh of relief as the gate closes and our chicks are safely back to roost.

Suddenly, while we weren't looking, time advanced too quickly, and we hold our hands to our hearts and hold our breath, dumbfounded; we watch and wave as our parental gate of opportunity and influence shuts. Oh, we know it is time and we tremble as we hang on loosely. The love of home, old friendships, and parental guidance will now surely be tested. It is off to college or a career and the roost has a vacancy—or perhaps, the nest is empty.

Life on the homestead goes on, immersed in daily routine, until one day the theme of normalcy is broken ... it happens in this story, as it did in my life, but remember—the good Lord is in charge and He is good, all the time. To God be the glory. Amen.

FUTURE TENSE

Listen intently and you can hear the tires of a shiny limo rolling down a gravel road. Imagine pebbles being spewed from the tire's broad tread, shelling tassel-topped weeds along the roadside, as it travels the bone-dry back country lane. Springtime verdant green is long gone, and it is summer, blistering hot. Dust devils dance behind the hand-polished black veneer of this sleek classy stretch. Even though the air inside is chilled to an acceptable 68 degrees, you are not mistaken if you see that an anxious sweat has formed on the brow of the single uptight passenger.

"How much longer, Jiles," the impatient man prodded the driver, "I believe you said this was to be a shortcut ... did you not?" The black pinstripe suit and conservative fedora man demonstratively began tapping the face of his expensive gold watch as if to shout, "Hey driver, you see this? My time is money, daylight's burning! You have no idea where we are, do you? You will be fired if we are not on time. We have to be on time—our contract obligates us!" But this little horn-rimmed glass man speaks not; he simply continues the annoying watch tapping in silence, his countenance as bleak as he considers the Texan landscape to be.

Meanwhile, in a quaint white clapboard steeple country church, not far from the approaching black limo, a girl just beyond the age of twenty-three addresses its congregation and visitors. She is "Lady Parsons," a singer/songwriter who today is delivering a hopeful message and introducing a praise-time song. "And God said, 'Behold I am coming quickly' ... And God shall wipe away all tears. He has wiped away my human stain, yet today, I confess that I am still a work in progress ... how about you?"

Now entering the outskirts of a humble community, the fidgety man taps his briefcase impatiently, gazing at the town's various buildings, making audible mental notes, "Some in disrepair, others for sale, some for rent or lease—oh, there's one all fixed up and open for business.

Aren't people just like this little burg? Oooops, there's one for sure ... CONDEMNED!"

"You say something, sir?" the driver asked.

"Not a word, Jiles, I spoke not a word," answered the man smugly.

Lady continues, "We all have our stories to share and mine is: I am nobody trying to tell everybody about Somebody who came to earth, lived as we do, died for everyone, and on the third day was raised up in order to save us, the undeserving people of this world. Amen.

The song I am about to play I wrote for a dear friend of mine; in a letter to me, they requested that it not be dedicated to them but rather to our Savior and Lord Jesus Christ. I have done as requested, and every note and bar played and sung hereafter is praise to the promise that Jesus made to you and me."

The man in the limo raved on to the driver, "Jiles, this town—or city—as the sign calls itself, must be the end of the line for all nobodies? Can you even imagine the sign also displays the boast, 'The Best Little City in Texas'! What brainiac came up with that drivel? This is awful, Jiles ... this dust and dirt hangs on me like a cheap suit and I have not set one foot outside yet. Not a word shall you say to anyone that we have even been here. I am sure the associates back at the tower are having a real hoot over this. I don't know what I have done to deserve such treatment. Not a word Jiles, not a word!"

Back at the church, Lady's monologue picks up, "The good Lord looks down on us with compassion. He sees us not as others see us, not as we see ourselves, and not as we have been, but rather He sees us in the light of what we may become.

I believe that we live two lives while here on earth—the one we experience and learn with, and the second, what we do with that knowledge once it is acquired. Some folks will accept it and pay it forward. Others will hide their newly found light and, sadly, there are the ones that just don't get it."

Finally, reaching their destination, the door of the limo swings open, almost ejecting the impatient man from the vehicle. Briefcase in hand, he leaps and bounds up the steps of the church, bursting open the front door. The ushers tell him to be quiet and have some respect for the sanctuary.

The man grumbles and again points to his watch, but the ushers pay no mind as their attention is drawn toward the front of the church. Briefcase man squinted, trying to adjust his eyesight, and looked over at the seated congregation. He pulls from his jacket pocket a piece of paper and a photo and attempts to match them up to his person of interest.

Lady, now seated at the piano, speaks out, "For in the beginning was the Word and the Word was with God. And His promise is that wherever two or more are gathered in His name—'Emanuel—God with us'—He will be there, also. Praise God! Here is the song, "The Promise."

STARTING AT THE BEGINNING

The song ended and Lady got up from the piano. She was in a studio in Los Angeles, California, and had placed the finishing touches on its arrangement. Walking back to the engineer's booth, she asked the three seated gentlemen who were listening, "What do you think?"

Producer Harriman spoke first, "That song needs to be heard ... it delivers what people are looking for—hope and promise."

The engineer chimed in, "Just notes and words on paper until you gave them flight and a purpose, if you want my opinion."

Lady gently touched the engineer's shoulder, "Of course I do, and respect your opinion." She turned to her old friend and music coordinator, Will, and asked, "How did it feel to you, Will—do you think Jesse would like it?"

"Aahh, Lady, the melody reached the gates of heaven; truth be told, this day has been a long time comin'.'"

Tears could be seen in Lady's eyes, and she shook her head, "When he needed me most, I wasn't there."

"You've turned lemons into lemonade by handing it up to the Lord. Just listen to what you've accomplished."

"Am I missing something here?" Producer Harriman jumped in, sounding a bit cranky, "Thought this was a praise song. What's with all the sadness—move on with the overdubs already!"

"Can't—no, I won't," Lady rebuked, "Perfection can't be bought!"

"We're on the clock, Lady," Harriman warned, "Don't need any diva drama today."

"It's your dime," Lady replied and raised her voice, "How could we forget, as you tell us every minute? But all notes played, all words sung, I am personally accountable for their conclusion. Music is *the* most powerful influence. David calmed King Saul's demons with it. Angels sing praises to God unceasingly. There's an entire book in the Bible called *Psalms*—praises to God—set to music, maybe you should check it out?"

Attempting to calm the stirring waters of anguish, Will advised, "Lady, maybe Harriman should hear your story as to why there is such a veil of emotion concerning this song?" Now turning to Harriman, Will questioned, "You're a believer, aren't you Harriman ... at least you claim to be?"

A veil of condescension was raised as Harriman answered, "Of course I am ... I mean, how can I not be? It's the line of business we're in. What a question!"

> "Lady, maybe Harriman should hear your story as to why there is such a veil of emotion concerning this song?"

"Ah-ha, okay then," Will considered Harriman's somewhat ambiguous answer and asked, "All for business, really? Good, then for once can we leave time in God's hands?"

Shrugging his shoulders, Harriman agreed but couldn't help looking at his watch as he glibly said, "Okay, fine. I am already seated; ramble, if you must."

"Cannot tell the story, Harriman, without starting at the beginning, or confessing my own transgressions," Lady stated. "Jesse, my friend ... LA's not his kind of town ... but for me, being Texan, I am his number one fan. Jesse was not swayed by gold or fame, yet he understood my journey."

A TIME AGO

"Being fifteen or sixteen back then ... feels like it was another lifetime," Lady recalled, "I was seated on a blanket, humming out a tune beneath a shady oak tree on that beautiful morning, writing in my poetry book. Suddenly there were twigs dropping from the branches above; that forced me to look up. I thought it must be a squirrel or some other creature. I was right—it was some other creature."

"Hey, boy, what are you doing in my tree?" Lady called out.

"Ain't your tree ... my tree! I found it and besides, I was here first," Jesse called out as he started to climb down.

"That don't make it so," Lady replied. "I think it's my poppa's tree because it's his ranch. But I'll tell you what, boy. I'm willing to share. I'll do that much because my momma said that's the right thing to do."

"Okay, cool. It's a deal," the boy responded, and then asked, "Do you come here a lot?"

"Whenever I have time and when I'm not doing chores," Lady replied, and asked, "How about you? Do you come here often?"

Picking at the bark on the tree, the boy appeared shy and nervous as he answered, "Ah, whenever I get a break from helping out my old man. I come over here, where it's peaceful just to think on things."

Looking sideways at him and noting the cute shyness, Lady asked with a smile, "So what do I call you, other than boy?"

Perking up, he replied, "My name's Jesse ... and, and what's yours?"

"Lady ... my name's Lady," Lady answered, offering her hand to shake.

Looking shyly at her hand, Jesse at first didn't know what to do, but he quickly grasped hold and gave it a shake as he said, "Cool, very cool and I'm glad ... I mean I'm very glad to meet you. But I have to ask, what kind of name is 'Lady'? I mean no offense, but I never heard that one before."

Laughing a little at Jesse's awkwardness, Lady explained, "My dad had a very winning horse and could not help but saddle me with that awful name—Lady. I mean, what parent would do that? How did you come by your name?"

Pretending that his hands and forefingers were two loaded pistols, Jesse pointed them at her and mimicked shooting, "BANG! BANG! I'm Jesse James." Then he blew across each imaginary barrel.

Folding with laughter, Lady called out, "You got me—you got me! That's just too cute there, Jesse James! And we'll leave it at that."

Now embarrassed, Jesse looked at the ground, kicked a few pebbles, and said, "I'm sorry, guess I should get on back to the house before I'm missed."

Drying the tears of laughter, Lady asked, "Where is that—where do you live?"

"Just over this hill, not far from you is where we live," Jesse replied.

"You mean right there, really?" Lady asked.

"Yeah, thought you would have known that," Jesse speculated. "Your dad's what some of the old biddies call 'horsey people' cause y'all moved here from Kentucky, right?"

"Well, I guess you know all the news, huh?" Lady quipped. "Guess you're not sure 'bout me now, being that I am a 'horsey people'?"

Lady's twin brother, Hank, was hiding out behind a nearby tree, listening to the conversation.

In an attempt to smooth over what appeared to be a misunderstanding, Jesse backpedaled. "Nah, I like you a lot; it's those busybodied nosey people I don't like."

Out from behind the tree came Hank. "Hey, you don't like her? Then why are you hanging around here?"

Recoiling, somewhat on the defense, Jesse questioned, "Hey, who's this guy?"

Laughing at her brother's antics, Lady said, "Sorry for my brother's intrusive behavior, Jesse. Let me introduce you to my goofy twin brother, Hank."

Smiling at Jesse, Hank offered his hand as he said, "Hey pard, any friend of my sister is a friend of mine."

Jesse put out his hand, but Hank quickly pulled away, asking, "You are her friend, aren't you?"

"Hank!" Lady scolded, "don't be rude, you goofball!"

"Well of course I am," Jesse replied.

"Good, then we'll shake on it," Hank concluded. Jesse signaled that he had to get going, but Hank stopped him. "Whoa there, pard, I came over here because Momma sent me to get Lady for lunch, but since she's so sweet on ya, why not come along for the vittles? Lady can introduce you to the folks."

Throwing a stick in Hank's direction, Lady spoke up. "Hank, you are presumptuous and just being a clown. Maybe Jesse got chores or something else to do. Besides, you are embarrassing him."

"By now I am sure my dad's looking for me, so it is best I get going. But thanks for the invite, maybe some other time, though," Jesse said. "It was nice meeting both of you."

"Some other time," Lady added with a smile and held out her hand. "Let's shake on that!"

"Yeah, I'd like that," Jesse said, taking her hand. As he did, he felt a small piece of paper being pressed into the palm of his hand.

"I'll be back here soon, Jesse James," Lady called out, pointing a finger at him.

Waving goodbye, Jesse headed home.

Lady got up on the horse she had tethered to a tree. Hank took the reins and walked the horse, with Lady in the saddle, back to the ranch.

"You know that boy?" Lady asked her brother.

"Sorta … guess I do," Hank replied. "I see him at the lumber yard where Poppa buys his fence. He does help his dad. They do renovations and additions. His dad is really bossy from what I can tell—bordering on kinda rude, I think."

"Hey, Hank!" Lady exclaimed, pointing toward the house. "There's Momma! She's gonna ring that dinner bell."

The bell began to ring.

"Yessiree, now it's official," Hank observed. "She loves to do that—lunch must be ready!"

Hank and Lady both laughed.

JESSE DEFINED

As he walked over the hill to go home, Jesse was feeling very happy about his chance meeting. An even wider grin followed when he opened the note and read, *Call me sometime*! There was also a phone number.

"Yes!" was his response.

He now heard his father, Chester, loading up the truck with lumber and tools.

Approaching, Jesse could tell by his expression that Chester was in a mood, "There you are, boy. I could have used your help an hour ago. Where you been all this time? And you came sneaking out of the woods like you're hiding something?"

"I wasn't sneaking," Jesse assured him and answered, "I was hanging out with some new friends just over the hill—They're nice kids."

"That's where those newcomers, the 'horsey people' live, ain't it?" Chester asked. "Ain't no friends of mine, noses so high, they drown when it rains. What were you doin' over there?"

"Nothin' but talkin's all," Jesse answered.

"Sounds like a whole lotta talkin' goin' on," Chester smugly speculated. "These parrots got names?"

"They're not parrots, Dad, they're kids," Jesse answered, "and they're names are Hank and Lady. They're twin brother and sister."

"Now that you're here, make yourself useful and hand me a beer out of the cooler," Chester demanded.

"Come on, Dad, you know Momma doesn't like you to …" but he was cut off by his dad's gruff comment.

"And what, your little black book—your B-I-B-L-E tells you to think less of me?" Chester suggested. "Doesn't it say to respect your momma and poppa? Isn't that one of the special commands? And if it is, then crack me open a cold one!"

"Yessiree, it does say to respect," Jesse answered and headed for the ice chest. He took out a beer, popped the top, and reluctantly handed it to his dad.

"There ya go, boy, now you're helping the old man keep his sanity," Chester said, and suggested, "Maybe you should take the hair of the dog. It'd help make a man outta ya. Maybe help ya lasso that little filly across the hill from us."

"Yes, sir," Jesse answered, hoping to appease his dad.

"Atta boy." Chester smiled, sauntered off, and got into his pick-up. He took another swig and wiped his mouth with the back of his sleeve.

"I thought you needed my help today," Jesse called out.

"Not today, boy. I'm just finishing up a job to get paid," Chester answered and then added, "Momma took chemo today, so be quiet and hang around—might need your help as she looks and feels awful."

Jesse now got an empty feeling. To his dad, payday meant the bar and whatever that social event brought his way. "Okay, Pop," Jesse said. "Please don't be gone too long. There are some things I can't do for Momma and you know she gets mighty sick."

"You can handle it till I get back, boy," Chester said. "You are the man while I'm gone. Hang tough, and I'll see ya later."

Taking another sip of beer, Chester released the brake, let the truck roll down the driveway, and popped the clutch. The engine sprang to life; he guided the truck around the corner and was gone.

Eyeing the cooler, Jesse walked over and opened the lid. As he peered inside, he saw the cans floating on ice. Hesitating at first, at last he reached in and pulled out a can. He heard his poppa's words, "Make yourself useful, get me a cold one—maybe you should take some hair of the dog—make a man outta ya."

Popping the top, he smelled it, stopped, and then took a sip. Grimacing at the foreign taste, Jesse spat out the strange brew. Pouring out the remainder, Jesse tossed the can to the ground and crushed it under foot. After completing the act of defiance, he threw it into the trash can, looked to the sky, and called out, "Thank you, Lord!"

Deep in thought, Jesse looked at the garage, snapped his fingers as a mental light turned on, and walked inside. From a shelf he picked up an old dusty acoustic guitar he had found in the dumpster of one of the houses he and his dad renovated. He brushed the dust away from the tuning head and it revealed the letters G-i-b-s. The rest of the letters seemed to have been worn off, and he saw that it was missing one of the tuning heads. There was minor cracking in the finish on the body, and the strings were totally rusted.

He thought out loud, "But hey, I think she'll like this once I clean it and put some new strings on it. And I'll order a new tuning head from the music store in town." Grabbing some linseed oil and an old rag, feeling proud, he went over to the workbench to start the project.

But work was cut short as he heard his momma calling out, "Jesse, you there, honey! I need some help if you can."

Jesse went into the house and entered her bedroom. His mother, Ida, was propped up on some pillows and there was an open Bible on her lap.

She smiled courageously and said, "There's my brave young Jesse who has stood by me through fat and lean, and the good and bad of things. Please sit down here beside me, Son."

Jesse sat down in a chair close enough so that his mother tousled his hair and said, "I need to talk plainly to you Jesse, as I cannot lie. I am not long for this cruel world and there are things that need to be told."

"Aah, come on, Mom, the good old days are coming back; you'll be fit as a fiddle soon," Jesse said with a hopeful smile.

"Shhh, I know this is hard," Ida stated, "But about it all, I am at peace. I will soon be at rest in the arms of Jesus. There is encouragement in the Good Book. Read for me First Thessalonians chapter 4, verses 13 and 14, please."

Taking the Bible, Jesse read out loud, "But I would not have you to be ignorant, brethren, concerning them which are asleep, that ye sorrow not, even as others which have no hope. For if we believe that Jesus died and rose again, even so them also which sleep in Jesus will God bring with Him."

"No, no! Momma, please!" Jesse lamented. "I can't do this, you, you …"

Reaching out, Ida gently touched Jesse's tearing face. "There, there, Son, don't waste a tear on me. Be strong. If you must cry out, pray for your dear father, who has taken no time for understanding. You are a light to this dark world. Promise me that you will pay forward in your deeds and actions the teachings of our Lord and Savior Jesus."

> "There, there, Son, don't waste a tear on me."

Touching his chin, Ida lifted up his head so that his eyes met hers. "Will you promise me that?"

He answered, "I promise you, Mom, with all my heart."

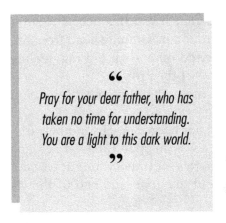

> *Pray for your dear father, who has taken no time for understanding. You are a light to this dark world.*

Satisfied, Ida took a deep breath and said, "There it is, then. Let's get down to the business at hand." Ida commanded, "Open the drawer in my nightstand and hand me the brown envelope from inside."

Doing as asked, Jesse inquired, "Ma, what is this?"

With as much strength as she could muster, Ida asserted, "Your future—let no one see this, especially your father. Put it somewhere close and safe. Do not open it until … well, until I have passed. Then give it to an attorney or magistrate. They will know what to do per my instructions, postmortem. Everything has been registered at the court, fully legal and all."

With doubtful concern, Jesse mumbled, "Momma, I don't know if I … "

"Yes, yes, you are Jesse, you are ready for this," Ida assured him and continued, "And I am plumb tuckered out. Git off with ya, but give me a good hug first."

Jesse got up and hugged his mom and as he began to walk away, he hesitated. "I met two really nice people today, just over the hill. They are from that ranch. Their names are Hank and Lady … that is truly her name—*Lady*. And ya know what?"

"What, my dear?" Ida asked with a smile.

Smiling back, feeling kind of silly, Jesse stated proudly, "Lady gave me her phone number."

"See, there ya go. You are on your way to living —give her a call, why don't ya," his mother suggested.

After Jesse left the room and Ida heard the back door close properly, she broke into tears and began to pray.

A BIBLE-VERSE SHOOTOUT, A BAPTISM, AND A FAIR

Morning broke on the Parsons' ranch. Months have flown by since Lady and Jesse first met. She has been quickly making Jesse her newest, best friend since meeting at their tree. In a hurry now, hardly touching the stairs, Lady saw her momma preoccupied with breakfast dishes. The faint aroma of pancakes and eggs lingered in the air and gave way to hint that there might be something left to forage.

"Well good morning to you, too," Momma called out.

"Sorry, Mom, I guess I overslept," Lady replied.

"Did you sleep all right. Anything wrong?"

"Slept like a rock, everything's great," Lady answered.

"Missed your dad and Hank—they went on over to the mill. Hank has mentioned a boy you've been keeping company with lately. In fact, he says that you've been seeing him for several months now. And right under our noses, or is that an oak tree," Momma prompted as she questioned.

"Guess so," Lady said, evasively.

"You can define that with a yes or no," Momma continued. "It is either no, have not—or yes, you have been seeing a boy."

"Well, I guess I do … his name is Jesse," Lady answered. "But we're just good friends, Momma, and that's all."

"Oh, Chester James's son," Momma said.

"Oh my," Lady murmured sheepishly, "I had never asked, because I thought it was a joke! His name really is Jesse James? I was just content with calling him Jesse. Oh, wow! Well, how would I know? He does go to another school. And I am mostly home schooled."

Momma rolled her eyes and thought, *Defense!*, and delivered a tepid breakfast. "No joke—how can you be so naïve? Did you not think to ask—

oh, I guess you have fallen so for this boy that it didn't cross your mind to care if he had a last name or not? And don't forget, you have a piano lesson at eleven."

Biting into cold toast, Lady grimaced and said, "Oh, by the way—I'd rather play guitar. And I canceled today's lesson. I need some time to think further about the piano. Like, I've been doing this since I was six; I can play just about anything. I need to move on."

"Another astounding revelation this morning," Momma quipped. "I don't know if I can take much more of this information overload. And if that is what you want, you must also keep up the piano lessons. Besides, you do not have a guitar. Good ones are not cheap, ya know."

"Yes, Momma," Lady replied, unconvinced.

"Let's get back to the real subject," Momma demanded, "What's with this boy? And did you know he is a year older than you? Or did you care not to ask?"

"He's only a junior. It's not like he's old enough to vote or anything. And well, he's kinda funny and cute," Lady replied, smiling, crunching another bite of cold toast while taking a mental drift. "He's sorta shy, too, in a boyish kinda way."

"You're only sixteen and shouldn't be thinking cute or anything else about boys," Momma warned. "No need to go and make your life complicated; plenty of time for foolishness later. Besides, he doesn't come from the best of surroundings."

"He says his dad drinks too much," Lady defended, "but what does that mean to me? Jesse is not that way."

"His father drinks and plays around with other women while his poor wife lies sick in bed," Momma related. "She's clinging to the shady side of life by a thread and Jesse is left to deal with her while his father plays the fool. I am just telling you there are problems over there, and yes, Jesse might be an angel, but I don't want anything affecting you adversely. Understand?"

Deep in contemplation of what her momma had just related, Lady looked down at her plate and pushed the food around with a fork. Jesse never told her about his mother's illness.

"Has the cat got your tongue?" Momma asked. "Your father and I just want the best for you, honey. We love you and care about you. You must understand that when everything goes wrong you can always count on family—remember that. No matter what happens, we will always be here for you."

Finally, Lady spoke. "I know Momma … I know how much you and Poppa care about me. I'm just thinking about Jesse's situation—it is so sad. How can anyone, his father that is, just give up on someone they once claimed to care so much about?"

"Whoever said that life is fair?" Momma advised, "Hank said that he thinks that boy is nice enough. But don't take on something that will become painful, or that you will regret later."

"Also, dear Lady, the county fair is approaching—like the middle of next month. You are to be singing backup, and you have two songs of your own that you are leading out on. Remember … you, who was the prize winner of the talent show?"

Lady replied, "I am so, so ready. I wonder who I am singing backup for."

"Oh, one of those roadshow people who travel all around to county fairs and such," Momma answered, then added, "I think it's that guy 'Slo' Hand Scottie.' I saw him a while back. He's pretty entertaining. He'll have his own backup band with him, too. Should be a hoot."

"Slo' Hand Scottie, saw him a while back … really … how old's this guy … should be a hoot all right," Lady said, not amused. She added, "I hope I get to practice with these so-called roadshow people."

"The day of the show, I was told, you will get to meet, greet, and sing like a birdie," Momma chirped. "Your poppa and I, along with Hank, will take you over to the rehearsal just to make sure it is all on the up and up. We are to be there around one o'clock. Seems these musician types can't get up too early. Waste of the best part of the day, as I see it."

The ring of the telephone broke the conversation, and Lady sprinted to answer. "Hello." There was a pause on the other end. Lady continued, "I hear you breathing, jokester. Is this one of those prank calls where you say, 'I saw what you did' … well, I will find you … my poppa will whup you into some kinda pudding. I'm gonna hang up now."

"No wait, hold on, it's me!" Jesse responded nervously.

"Oh, it is the squirrel who likes to toss twigs into Lady's hair," Lady guessed. "I don't normally talk to squirrels but … because it is nonsense Thursday, I will accept. What's up, tree varmint?"

"You gave me your phone number, remember?" Jesse stated.

Teasingly, Lady responded, "Who, me? Did I do that, Mr. Jesse James? This is like the first time you used it, Mister-About-Time. You want to meet at our tree in fifteen so we can shoot it out?"

Jesse's short answer sufficed. "Yup!"

Lady sat on the bench next to the back door, put on her cowgirl boots, and grabbed her 4/10 single-barrel shotgun.

"Well, suddenly you're in a hurry. Got your shotgun, too, I see," her momma observed, and added, "That's good, you can never be too careful ya know … snakes crawlin' or walkin'!"

They both laughed at that.

"Thanks, Momma, and I know to be careful," Lady answered and paused to ask, "I'll take Silky out for a ride and go over to the oak tree? I'd like to go out before it gets too hot."

"Okay, if that makes you happy," Momma said. "At least by the phone call I know who you're meeting. But remember to tighten those cinches; watch out for the rattlers and gopher holes."

"I know, I know, I know," Lady called out over her shoulder.

The vapor trail passed Momma as she attempted to get in the last word before the screen door slammed, "Make sure the gun is loaded—it don't work if it ain't!"

Waiting at the tree was Jesse, as Lady rode up. Seeing her shotgun he exclaimed, "Whoa, girl, you weren't kidding about a shootout! But look at what I have—my Bible. Exodus 20:13, 'Thou shalt not kill.' That's one of the Ten Commandments."

"Okay, you want a Bible-verse shootout—Deuteronomy 5:17, Mr. B-I-B-L-E!" Lady challenged.

Jesse replied, "Again, 'Thou shalt not kill' ...how clever of you ... it is part of the Decalogue, the covenant that God made with Moses for the children of Israel. A scriptural shootout, okay."

"Hit me with your best shot, Jesse James," Lady dared.

Jesse paused and then asked, "What is the most well-known Bible verse, and it must be quoted."

"Silly boy, no problem," Lady responded. "John 3:16, 'For God so loved the world, that he gave his only begotten Son, that whosoever believeth in Him should not perish, but have everlasting life.' And let's include the game changer, John 3:17, as well, 'For God sent not his Son into the world to condemn the world; but that the world through him might be saved.'"

Taking a bow, Lady stated, "Ha, my turn!"

Jesse bowed and waved his arm gracefully, "I give Lady the floor."

In a teasing tone Lady quipped, "'And he said, I am the voice of one crying in the wilderness, make straight the way of the Lord.' And who predicted this event?"

Quickly Jesse replied, "Too easy, book of John 1:23. John the Baptist talking to the Jewish priests when they asked him who he was!"

Smugly folding her arms, Lady came back with, "Wrong-o, Mr. Jesse. It was the prophet Isaiah in his book, Chapter 40, verse 3. 'The voice of him that crieth in the wilderness, prepare ye the way of the Lord, make straight in the desert a highway for our God.' It is what is needed today in this spiritual desert. I won!"

"Sneaky, very sneaky," Jesse accused. "That was a trick question. You should be thinking of the golden rule. Do unto others as you would have them do unto you; love thy neighbor as thyself, hmmm? That would be book of John, chapter 13, verse 34."

Lady apologized. "Okay, I agree. But you answered too quickly. As we both know, John the Baptist knowingly quoted Isaiah when he spoke to the Jewish priests. Let's have a seat under our tree."

"Where did you learn so much scripture?" Jesse asked.

"Every Saturday morning we have Bible study at the ranch," Lady explained. "You need to come around. We are getting a few people to study with us. Where do you get your influence?"

"My mother has me reading to her every day," Jesse answered. "She has cancer, been fighting it for a long time and, sadly, she feels that it will soon be over. It cuts me deep in my heart, but for her, maybe it is best that she finds peace."

"Oh dear, I am so sorry," Lady said sympathetically. "If there is anything I or my family can do, just ask. I had heard something, but why didn't you tell me about this before?"

"I don't like to say much about me personally," Jesse confessed and added, "You can pray for Momma. There's power in that, and I trust in that for certain. Maybe you could come with me to church in a few weeks. I've been studying with Pastor Richards. I am getting ready to be baptized and it would be an honor to have you witness."

"You are full of surprises," Lady said with compassion, taking Jesse's hand in hers. "You just melted my heart. I would be honored to be at your baptism."

Two weeks flew by, and Lady found herself and twin brother Hank sitting in his pick-up truck in front of a small white clapboard country church. The hymn "Shall We Gather at the River" could be heard coming from inside.

"You sure about all this, Lady?" Hank queried.

"I know, I know what Momma said about being unequally yoked," Lady explained. "I feel compelled. I want to do this for Jesse. His mother is here and still alive. What a blessing that the Lord has seen to keep her present for this blessed event. It's important, Hank. Let's go."

"Under Momma's nose ... okay." Hank laughed and pressed on, "Let's do this, Sis. We'll ask for forgiveness, if need be, after the fact."

"Amen and amen," Lady said with a wry smile.

As Lady and Hank entered the church, an usher seated them at the back. On the platform stood Pastor Richards and three teens, two boys and a young lady. Jesse was among them. He spotted Lady and smiled.

An elderly lady was up front sitting in a wheelchair. Lady assumed that was Jesse's mother. She had a hanky in her hand and was shedding tears of happiness. It was soon Jesse's turn, and Pastor Richards held up his hand for the congregation to pause from their singing.

Pastor Richards spoke to the people. "This is a very special day for all of us, and the angels in heaven are rejoicing as well. It was brought to my attention by a very special request. I decided to grant her wish. Lady Parsons, I see you have arrived. Would you please come forward?"

Surprised, Hank looked at Lady. "Really, Sis, what are you doing?"

"I got this, it's okay Hank," Lady assured.

Lady stood up and people rubbernecked to see who it was that stopped the program. Lady came up front and an usher handed her a microphone. The pianist nodded to her that she was ready.

"Hi, I am Lady Parsons," she began. "Jesse did not know I was going to do this. He simply requested that I be here. And I will be brief as I know they are standing in water. I do hope it is heated."

There were chuckles from the congregation.

"I called Mrs. James to find out Jesse's favorite hymn," Lady explained. "Thank you, Mrs. James, for being discreet."

Mrs. James acknowledged with a wave of her hanky and smiled.

"With the Lord's blessing, I will sing "In the Garden" as Jesse is reborn into Christ Jesus," Lady said.

The pianist began to play, and Lady spoke over top of the music; "And Jesus answered, truly, truly I say unto you, unless one is born of water and spirit, he cannot enter the kingdom of God." Lady paused and then began to sing. "I come to the garden alone, while the dew is still on the roses. And the voice I hear falling on my ear, the Son of God discloses." Lady prompted the congregation to join ... "And He walks with me and he talks with me and He tells me I am His own; and the joy we share as we tarry there, none other has ever known." And all the congregation joined in the *amen*.

With the conclusion of the baptism, the congregation began to file out of the sanctuary. Lady saw Mrs. James sitting alone and went over to give her a hug. They had met only in a brief telephone conversation.

Bursting with praise, Mrs. James said, "What a blessing you are, young lady, and I don't mean it as a pun. You hold inside of you the voice of angelic authority. You need to be heard."

"Praise the Lord. To God be the glory," Lady stated and said, "I want to introduce my twin brother Hank. Mrs. James, Hank. Hank, this is Jesse's mother, and I am so sorry ... I don't know your first name."

"Ida is my name," Mrs. James stated. "I am pleased to meet you, twin brother Hank. If you have half the voice of Lady ...."

"No, Ms. Ida," Hank assured, "I couldn't carry a tune even if it was wrapped up in a hay bale. She's the gifted one in that department."

"Well, so you say. But you have a talent for description," Ida declared, and then turned her attention, "Here comes my reborn son, Jesse. Praise the Lord!"

Pointing at Lady, Jesse quipped, "Sneaky, very sneaky. Now who is melting hearts?"

Giving his mother a big hug, Jesse looked to the back of the church and saw his father standing there. Jesse looked at his mother and said, "I didn't know that Dad was here."

"Oh, but Jesse, he wouldn't come with me," Ida said.

Everyone turned to look, but Chester had already disappeared. "He was there. I know it was him, he was there."

"Okay, I believe you. But now he's not. Forget about that and give this young girl a hug because she deserves it," Ida stated firmly.

"Yes, make it a big hug; she planned this whole thing by herself," Hank said, offering a handshake.

Jesse turned his attention to Lady, who was standing close by ... opened his arms and said, "You have gone above and beyond. This was so thoughtful and kind. Thank you for making this day so special."

They embraced, and Lady said again, "To God be the glory ... amen." And they all responded, "Amen!"

"Hank! Lady!" Mrs. Parsons gave marching orders to the two teens. "Not past ten o'clock do I want to hear you pull up outside. I sleep with one eye open, and I can hear an ant walking the tall grass. No way ... not like last week when Hank came in on what he considered 'the stealth mode'—engine off, lights out—and coasted in the drive.

Didn't say nothin' then 'cause you were the lone dog. Hear me now, Hank Parsons! Loud and clear, I say. That is my precious one you are carrying tonight—your only sister. Hearin' me?"

"Loud and clear as your dinner bell, Momma," affirmed Hank. "And you can be Texas certain I take care of our own."

Second: My pies and jams—check on them, please," mamma asked and cautioned, "I don't want the old bait-and-switch going on by the busybodies. I am certain to win something. Because we are the newbies, the vein of envy runs deep. Don't trust many of these old biddies."

"Got your back, Momma," Lady said. "I'd know your baked goods blindfolded."

"And also, Lady, tomorrow is your singing debut. All that said, off with ya now." She added with a sniffle, "Guess I just don't like seeing my kids growing up so fast."

Going out the front door, the two youths jumped into Hank's newly acquired pick-up and went down the driveway to a night of freedom.

With a mischievous smile, Lady beamed and began to ramble, "I can't believe that Poppa actually gave you his pick-up truck. How cool is this? So you snuck down the driveway last week? Is it true that you have been dating Hailie, what's her name, complete with an underbite and a dimple on her chin?"

She poked Hank's chin with her index finger. "On her chin, right there!"

Hank pushed her finger away and warned, "Knock it off—I'm trying to drive. I have to take care of you, ya know. Don't distract me or get me upset or I will turn this boat around and take the silliness home."

"So, it is true, Mr. Hanky Panky," Lady smiled, feeling full of herself on the discovery. "You know she lightens her hair and wears colored contacts—she's manufactured. Not au naturel like moi." Lady then batted her eyes and flipped her hands through her hair.

Laughing out loud, Hank responded, "You are such a cat!"

Claws were mimicked and Lady growled, "Ggrrrrwwlll! I am not a meow; I am a lioness ready to pounce."

Bright lights of the fair appeared ahead, music could be heard, and the smell of carny food wafted thick in the air. Hank asked as he pulled into a parking spot, "Okay, dear kitty cat, where's he hiding, and do I need to chaperone?"

Windows in the pick-up were open and Jesse stepped forward. "Nah, Hank, I can be her chaperone tonight."

A Bible-verse Shootout, a Baptism, and a Fair

Hopping out of the truck, Hank said, "Great, I can leave you alone with the cat-woman and I can go seek out my unnatural friend. Back here by 9:30, and don't be late, and Lady, check on Momma's food wares."

Lady got out of the passenger side, saluted Hank, "Yessiree, comandante!"

"What's up?" Jesse asked.

"There's a certain chick he has hidden. I called him on it, and he got peeved with me," Lady explained.

Laughing at Lady's dilemma, Jesse said, "Oh, Hailie with the underbite. It's common knowledge that Hank Parsons has been corralling her."

The two had a laugh and Jesse said, "Really she's okay ... smart too ... not my type, though."

Lady looked at Jesse, "And what or who is your type, young man?"

Quickly Jesse diverted the attention. "Oh look, there's one of those crazy photo booths. Let's make some crazy faces and get our pictures taken in the process."

Lady pulled Jesse along, "Let's! Come on, shy guy!"

Feeding money into the machine ... the photos started. Lady grabbed Jesse's face and started kissing it all over and quickly jumped out of the booth. Jesse, with photos in hand, got out to see Lady standing proud, arms folded, and sporting a catty smile. "Well that was fun!"

"You got me," Jesse admitted.

"All's fair, they say," Lady challenged. "Now answer my question. Who is your type?"

With back against the wall, Jesse gave it up, "You are, Lady ... you are all I think about."

Appeased, Lady grabbed Jesse's arm. "Correctamundo! You just won the prize! Let's go shoot some darts and win me a huge panda bear! But first, let's ride the big ferris wheel. It's bigger this year, should be really cool. We'll be able to see into tomorrow land from up there."

"I don't know, Lady, that thing's outta-sight high," Jesse faltered. But Lady pulled him on board and soon they were flying high above the madding crowd.

As the wheel went round, Lady took from her jean jacket some strawberry string licorice. She opened the packet and pulled out a piece.

Jesse looked at her and said, "I really like that stuff."

"Me, too," Lady agreed, and asked, "Would you like an end?"

"I would eat the whole pack if given the chance," Jesse stated.

"Not so fast, shy guy. You have to earn it!" Lady demanded.

"How so?" Jesse asked.

"I put one end in your mouth. The other is mine and we meet in the middle. And if it is worth the journey, we share the whole pack," Lady answered.

"If not?"

"I throw you off the ferris wheel," Lady laughed. "So here we go." She placed one end in Jesse's mouth and the other in hers. They met in the middle and kissed just as the ferris wheel stopped at the top, sending the carriage rocking. They held each other tight.

Lady whispered into Jesse's ear, "That was the best, sweetest licorice kiss I could have imagined."

Jesse pulled away and looked into Lady's eyes. "I would have never imagined."

The ferris wheel jerked into motion and Lady saw the stage where she would perform and said, "Jesse, I want you to be here tomorrow when I perform with a roadshow band. You can come with us. It is so important to me that you be here. I want you to see what it is that I want to do with my career as a performer."

"Of course I will be here. That would be so cool," Jesse agreed. "I can walk over to the farm and go from there."

"It is a date," Lady smiled and added, "Don't be late!"

Hand in hand they got off the big wheel, walked along, chatted, took in the fairway lights, and of course, carny food. Lady took the conversation to a serious point, "So what are you planning to do with your life, Jesse James?"

Lady suddenly burst into song, "Because I want a mansion, just over the hilltop. In a bright land where I'll never grow old." She bowed comically.

> "For you, Lady, I will build that mansion," Jesse affirmed. "I don't know how yet, but the Lord will provide."

"For you, Lady, I will build that mansion," Jesse affirmed. "I don't know how yet, but the Lord will provide."

"You promise?" Lady asked.

"Yes, Lady," Jesse assured her, "I PROMISE! And to your bigger question, since you asked—I want to help the less fortunate. Have a place where kids from the city can come and kids from broken homes would find sanctuary. Help them to rebuild, enjoy nature, teach them about the Bible and how to trust in the Lord rather than the world."

Lady thought for a minute and clarified, "So you want to build a place, a Bible-based life skills learning center for the less fortunate. Lift them up, centered on the teachings of Jesus. That is, to me, a fabulous idea."

"I pray to God to make that happen," Jesse said, adding, "And it would be great if I had someone to share that dream with."

"`Yes, you would need a life pardner." Lady now embraced his arm and put her head on his shoulder and continued, "A life pardner with the same ideals and goals. Both share the same passion for Bible principles."

Thunderstruck, millions of feelings were ebbing inside of Jesse as he listened to Lady's words, and all he got out was, "Yes, I love you, and what you are saying ... ."

Interrupted in thought, Lady blurted out, "Looky, there's that crazy dart game ... come on!"

Over the carnival noise and through the crowd Lady pulled Jesse hurriedly to the barker calling out, "EVERYBODY WINS! NO LOSERS HERE! EVERYBODY GETS A PRIZE. HEY THERE, YOU TWO, I CAN SEE YOU IN THE WINNERS' CIRCLE ... TWO DARTS, TWO BUCKS, FIVE FOR FOUR! COME ON, KIDS ... WHADDYA SAY?"

"We'll take five for four!" Jesse called out.

"We got a player here," the barker shouted, "You hit five, that's the money shot and the big prize!"

Gently Lady took the darts from Jesse and said, "Allow me, shy guy."

The barker shouted out, "Ah ha! The Lady wants to play! Good luck on this one!"

Winking at Jesse, Lady slowly rolled the darts in her hand, turned, winked at the big panda bear and said, "I gottcha sucker!" Then she threw the darts one after the other. Bang! Pop! Bang! Pop! She turned and winked at Jesse. Bang! "I will have the big panda bear now, Mr. Barker, sir!"

Now speechless, the barker motioned to his helper to retrieve the panda. Speaking up, the barker asked Lady, "Double or nothing?"

"You want me to own your dart stand?" Lady questioned.

"Oh, never mind," the barker replied and moved on. "NEXT! See ... right here a winner, every time, every time there's a winner!"

People standing around applauded as the panda was handed over to Lady.

"That's some gal you've got there, son," the barker leaned over and remarked.

"Don't I know it!" Jesse agreed.

Lady was hugging her prize and Jesse shook his head, blown away by Lady's dart expertise. He asked, "How in the world did you do that?"

"We have a dart board in the barn," Lady explained. "Hank and I have been throwing darts like forever. These carny barkers put weights in the darts to throw the players off. That's why I rolled them around in my hand. The last one was the worst, and a bit tricky, but thanks be. Here, you hold the panda. Let's go check on Momma's desserts."

The bear was almost as big as Jesse. People stopped and pointed. Kids gave the thumbs up sign and cast approving looks. "Cool bear," one person said. "You are the shooter," another commented.

"I'll not tell anyone if you don't. Cool—Jesse James the shooter," Lady chuckled, and they both laughed. "Over there is the contest hall and Momma's wares are near the entrance," Lady pointed out.

They entered the hall and Jesse said, "Smells great in here. Wish I could see what it was I was smelling."

Grabbing Jesse's hand, Lady chided, "Oh, man up! Hey, Momma won some prizes. Give me the bear so you can see."

Jesse began to sing, "I can see clearly now, the bear is gone. Mrs. Parsons won some prizes, too."

"You goof. First prize for her strawberry preserves. Woo hoo!" Checking her watch, Lady said, "Here, take the bear, we gotta go now. Walk me and the panda to the truck."

Already waiting, Hank called out, "Cool, right on time! Good work. And who is the freeloader?"

"Jesse won me this great big panda," Lady said. "Ain't he the cool one?"

"Quite the shooter there, dude," Hank said admiringly. "You will have to come over to the barn and play sometime."

"By the way, Hank," Lady commanded, "tomorrow Jesse's coming along to the roadshow. I invited him to see me perform. He will walk over to the ranch to join us."

"Or I can pick you up at your house," Hank said agreeably, and asked, "House? Ranch? Ranch? House?"

"Ranch house, if you don't mind," Jesse stated, chuckling at Hank's quick word play.

"Ranch it is. Say around six?" Hank asked.

"Cool," Jesse agreed.

Lady quickly grabbed the bear from Jesse and stuffed it in the truck and then in one motion pulled Jesse away and whispered. "Thank you,

Jesse, really. And I heard those three special magical words. Don't think that I didn't. I will see you tomorrow and then some."

An embrace ensued and Jesse whispered, "Thank you for hearing."

Slowly Lady released, looked him lovingly in the eyes, placed a kiss on her fingertips and touched his lips. "More than a licorice-kiss, shy guy. We are more than that, don't you know?"

Handing Jesse the remaining pack of the licorice, Lady said, "I didn't throw you off the ferris wheel, did I ... you won my heart. Don't break it or I'll bust your jaw."

Not another word was spoken.

Watching as the truck pulled away, Jesse pulled the photos from his pocket. Then he touched his lips and remembered what the steamy barker had said. "That's quite a gal you got there!"

Shouting out loud, "Don't I know it? Yes, I do!"

LADY MAKES A STATEMENT

Lunch dishes were washed, and Lady helped her mother by drying and putting them away. Her father noted this and asked, "A little nervous, Lady? You hardly ever dry and put things away. Trying to stay busy, eh?"

Lady dropped a pan and replied, "Who am I to be nervous?"

"What do you think, Dot?" Harlin asked his wife.

"Just a few jitters, I'd say," Mrs. Parsons replied.

Hank burst through the door, "Suburban fueled and ready for departure, Sir."

"Alrighty then, let's get a move on," Harlin said. "Time to let our songbird out of her cage."

The fair grounds were slightly different during the day, Lady noticed. "Seems so different, calm, not as many people about, but business as usual."

"People are a little more laid back. Coming more for the eats and the agricultural display barns," Hank observed and added, "Should have entered our prize bull, Poppa."

"Good luck with that, Hank," Harlin replied. "He's too mean. Almost crushed me in his stall. Remember, you had to keep me from shooting that no-good so and so."

"Yes, I remember, Poppa," Hank agreed. "Look, over there is Slo' Hand Scottie's trailer and it looks like the crew are sitting around a barbecue, playing music and singing."

"Smoking, too, I'd guess. Probably telling lies and unfit stories," Momma surmised, folding her arms.

"Come on, darlin'," Harlin pleaded. "We haven't even met them yet. What harm can this do?"

Dot calmed down a little and said, "Okay, but I am keepin' close watch as to what goes on. These musician types—can't trust 'em."

"It's okay, Momma," Lady said, trying to assure her mother. "I can hold my own when it comes to the street. I can watch out for myself; really, I can. Plus, I got big brother Hank watching my back."

"All right, sounds like you got more experience than you're lettin' on, Lady." Momma observed.

Lady sat back and gave Hank, who was driving, a wink via the rear view mirror. Hank smiled and said, "Look, I think that is Slo' Hand Scottie himself."

Upon leaving the vehicle, Slo' Hand came over to greet the Parsons family. "You all can call me Scottie. Everybody else does." He offered his hand to Harlin.

"Harlin is my name, my wife Dot, son Hank, and of course this is Lady, the talented one of the family."

"Pleased to meet you folks, and if y'all don't mind we will get right down to it and git our move on," Scottie suggested. "There are chairs for everyone and possible eats once Chef Lee gets it ready. Lady, there is a piano over there if you are so inclined. I understand you picked two songs for us to go over with you, and I have one for you to sing backup with me on. When we do that tonight, I will introduce you to the audience. Yes, folks, we roadshow hobos do have a plan." He looked at Mrs. Parsons and smiled.

Dot blushed a little and stammered, "Yes ... that is good ... a plan. If you don't have one you plan to fail," she affirmed.

"So before we get to my song where you will be singing backup, what are your tunes we need to go over?" Scottie asked.

Lady produced song sheets for everyone and began to hand them out. "Hold on there, Lady," Scottie cautioned, "can you play them on the piano? I got the musicians here and they are wantin' to cut loose. You give them the key and we have no fear of flyin', believe you me. That's Sour Hickle on fiddle, banjo, and steel; Geoff 'the Jet' Craven on keys and guitar; 'One Tom' John Erdley—percussion; Winsome Bruce Bozyk on bass; and Slo' Hand Scottie on lead guitar; and we are The Train Wreck Survivors."

"Nice to meet y'all! For sure ... I can play the piano just a little ... okay, cool," Lady stated as she sat down. "My two songs are 'I've Got a Mansion' and 'Country Roads.' I gave a lyrical twist to it, just for this occasion."

Momma had to respond, "Such a good idea," to Mr. Scottie.

Scottie nodded, noted, and smiled, "I am sure it is, Mrs. Parsons."

"But first, Mr. Slo' Hand," Lady stated as she kicked away the piano stool. She hit thunderous chords and roared to life,

"I quit my job and I changed my life;
   my folks said, you will barely survive.
   I got assorted commitments up to my ears;
   haven't been in one place for the last ten years,
   BUT I'VE GOT MUSIC AND LYRICS BURIED IN MY SOUL!
   Could be platinum, but they say it's gold,
   Nuthin' really more that I can do,
   but to keep on singin' these rhythm and blues …
Ba ba ba ba ba ba ba do-dee-dee, done!"

She stopped abruptly. Meekly, Lady picked up the piano stool, smiled at the numb and dumb onlookers, sat back down, and politely asked, "How about 'I've Got a Mansion' and 'Country Roads' now?"

Scottie, the Survivors, and Chef Lee, who was so surprised that he dropped his spatula, began to applaud. Hank just shook his head and smiled. Momma went ghostly pale, but Poppa applauded and shook his head knowingly. "This is a horse that can win the race."

The boys in the band and Slo'Hand Scottie proceeded with smiles and jumped confidently into rehearsal.

"Well now, Lady," Scottie said, grinning ear to ear, "I have some great ideas for tonight's show, if you would not mind and if your momma goes along with this. You see, the song I want you to sing backup on is called "Long Black Veil" by Lefty Frizzell. He was born close to here in Corsicana."

"I am familiar with it," Lady said, smiling.

"Great," Scottie replied. "So we start the song, and we have a dry ice effects machine that I have been wanting to use for the longest time. It produces what looks like smoke. We have you walk through that mist and it will look like you are floating onto the stage. You sing the chorus with me as you walk on. After that song, I introduce you to the world."

"Wow," Lady said. "What do you think, Momma?"

"You're asking me? It's your debut, your coming out, so to speak. I have some sheer black cloth that we can make into a veil for sure, head-to-toe length if that works for you, Mr. Scottie?"

"Now we're talkin'," Scottie answered. "Mrs. Parsons, that is a great idea. This rehearsal went fabulous and we will knock 'em dead tonight. If this goes as well as I think it will, there will be more opportunities, young lady, no pun intended ... and good pay, as well. I will relay this to Brad, my manager. What do y'all think, Parsons family?"

Poppa smiled and said, "As long as Momma is okay with it, I will agree. Let's see how tonight goes."

Hank slapped his knee, "Heck yeah, I knew Sis had the gift."

On the way back to the ranch Momma spoke her piece, "You have to know, Lady, that all you need is right here on the ranch. If there be peace in your heart and trust in the Lord, He will deliver His abiding love no matter where you choose to be. That is all I have to say about the matter."

"I am at peace, Momma, with it all," Lady assured. "I have this idea that I can make a difference and change lives by and through what gifts God has given me."

> "I have this idea that I can make a difference and change lives by and through what gifts God has given me."

Hank handed Poppa a flier. "Here, check this out."

Unfolding the paper, Mr. Parsons gave a whistle and said, "Well looky here. 'Slo' Hand Scottie and The Train Wreck Survivors featuring special guest star talent show winner Lady Parsons!'"

"And what would have happened today if I hadn't made the cut?" Lady speculated.

"You would have suddenly come down with the flu is my guess," Hank said with a laugh.

"You certainly put on quite the show in the beginning, young girl," said Momma. "Where'd you come up with all that sass? I never heard you banging on the keys and shouting like that in our house! Really, Lady, that just stunned ... no, it shocked me to here and gone. Thought I was ta take a heart failure! Really!"

"It's only rock 'n' roll, Momma," Hank said with a smile.

"I know what it is, but not in my house it's not," Momma stated. "Hhhhmmph."

Everybody laughed at Momma's certainty.

"Momma, I meant no offense, but felt I had to make a show that I was not a pushover, ya know, get some respect," Lady explained.

"She's right," Poppa agreed. "You have to give her some credit, Momma. We Parsons are a competitive lot."

"Oh, I suppose I'll give her that," Momma smiled and patted Lady's arm. "God has blessed you with that voice and I heard ya about wanting to play guitar. God will provide, is all I can say."

"Oh, by the way. I asked Jesse to come and see the show tonight," Lady said, adding sheepishly, "Could he come along with us? I don't think he has a way to get there."

"Wonderful opportunity," Momma replied. "I will get to meet the mystery guest who has been wooing my daughter under our old oak tree for God only knows how long."

Harlin laughed. "Oh, I have known about the young man. Good looking and stoutly framed from what I can tell from a distance …through my binoculars."

"How dare you, Poppa!" Lady exclaimed, not amused. "You've been spying on me!"

Again Harlin chuckled, "No dear, no. I would never do that. Quite by accident, really. I was over by my favorite fishing hole, looking for deer signs. Happened to be looking around and there you two were in my frame of sight. I must say you two make a nice couple. From what I could tell, you were reading from the Bible. Innocent, I assure you."

"Well okay then, Poppa, I believe you," Lady said, folding her arms just like her momma.

"At that, I would be happy as well to meet the young lad," Harlin agreed.

"Oh, by the way," Hank added, "this is for the cat-woman in the back seat. I will be picking up Hailee, the unnatural, to go along with us, as well. Please keep your claws to yourself, both verbal and otherwise."

"Meeooow," Lady replied cheekily, using her index finger to touch her chin. She showed Hank her response in the rearview mirror.

"You are too much," Hank stated. "I mean it, Lady—do not embarrass me."

"Just playin,' Hank," Lady responded.

"Alrighty then," Harlin observed, "Looks like we have a boat load of passengers bound for the fair tonight in support of Lady. At least we will be hootin and hollerin for ya, gal."

"I love you guys," Lady said, "for your wanting to be with me on my journey, accepting me with all my good and bad ... thank you so much." Then Lady got teary eyed and again folded her arms.

Poppa turned around and looked Lady in her eyes and Momma grabbed her arm. "You are our only daughter, flesh and bone. If we would not be here for you and praise God for the gift of you, what would that make us? If we claim the love of Jesus and follow him not, we are liars. We love you, Lady, and stand by you on the blessed rock of Jesus."

Momma and Hank both sounded out, "Amen!"

Lady gave Momma a hug and then hugged Poppa. I'd hug you too, Hank, but you're driving," she said.

Looking in the rearview, Hank gave a thumbs up and smiled. "I'm here for ya, Sis."

Five fifty-nine p.m. ... there came a young man knocking on the Parsons' ranch house door.

The door cracked open, showing eyes of mischievous intent. "He's here, everybody! The young man whom everyone has been wanting to meet. The man, the myth, the legend behind the old oak tree mystery, none other than Jesse James!"

"You are such a brat," Jesse said, even more nervous than when he'd first arrived.

The door became wide open and there stood Mr. and Mrs. Parsons. "I agree," said Mr. Parsons with a smile. "She can be at times. Please come in." Harlin offered his hand.

Next Mrs. Parsons held out her hand and said, "Pleased to meet you, young man. Don't let our Lady, always full of vinegar, make you feel uncomfortable. She always seems to be puttin' to the test so to speak, and that I am sure you know."

"Yes, sir, and yes, ma'am. I am pleased to meet you both." Jesse responded. He saw Lady standing off to the side, nodding her head and smiling, pleased with the moment.

"Oh look, right on time here comes Hank with the other newbie for us to meet," Harlin observed, "and Lady, you be nice."

Rolling eyes in Lady's direction, Momma did not have to say words. The message was received. "Yes, Momma, I will be on my best behavior."

Looking at Lady, Jesse smiled and moved closer to her.

"We will head out then," Harlin stated. "Plenty of room in the suburban."

Hopping out of the pick-up, Hank ran to the passenger door and opened it. As his passenger got out, he introduced her to the group. "Mom, Dad, Lady of course you know, and her friend, Jesse. This Hailie."

Everyone responded and Lady looked at Hank and scratched her chin with a smile. Lady said, "Hank, you're driving—Hailie can sit in the back with me. We can get to know each other better."

Hank gave Lady a look.

"Oh, that would be so cool, Hank," Hailie said and walked over beside Lady.

Harlin suggested, "Jesse, why don't you ride shotgun. Momma and I will sit in the coach. Hank, are the folding chairs … ?"

"Yes, sir, in the back," Hank answered, looking at Lady, who was grinning at him.

"Let's be off then," Harlin stated, "Don't keep the potential fans waiting, and getting all the good seats and eats."

Once at the fairgrounds, Hank headed for Mr. Scottie's camp, where the group would gather to get ready for the show. Lady and her entourage arrived. Slo' Hand Scottie's manager was there to greet them. "Ah, you folks must be Parsons. I recognize Lady from her photo," the manager said. "How forgetful of me. My name is Hastings. Brad Hastings."

"Pleased to meet you, Mr. Hastings, and that goes for all of us," said Harlin. "What would you have us do?"

"For you folks who will not be going on stage, you can sit stage side or have front row seats—on us," Hastings offered. "For the star of the show, we will prep her as to how and when she will make her entrance. Did you bring the veil?"

"Oh yes, Mr. Hastings," Momma said, as she handed it to him.

"This is so, so cool," Mr. Hastings said. "Scottie has been chomping at the bit to use his special effects. This is it, and Lady, tonight is your night to appear through the mist."

Clapping her hands, Hailie blurted out, "A star is born … and I can say that I know her."

"But of course you can," Hank said, trying to pull her to his side.

"Harry," Mr. Hastings called out to his gaffer, "get the comfy chairs for the Parsons entourage; I think five will suffice. Front row center, please—eats and drinks as well. Just tell Harry what you want. We will take care of it. And Lady, if you would come with me, we need to go over some details—get refreshed and quietly rehearse our entrance and music with the crew.

Jesse was dumbfounded at the bustle and looked longingly at Lady. She smiled and blew him a kiss as she was led away. The Parsons group was escorted to front and center.

"Wow. Comfy chairs at the fair?" said Hank. "Better than our folding chairs," he whispered to Poppa. "Everybody else has the cheap seats."

Noticing Jesse's sad look, Harlin suggested, "Jesse, why not sit here beside me, and Hank sit beside Jesse? We men will be sandwiched between the roses."

There were singers and performers from local high schools on stage. One after another came and went. The audience applauded politely for their endeavors. A waitress showed up, just as Mr. Hastings had promised. She took the entourage's requests and quickly delivered.

Hank had to say something—rubbing his hands together, "I am hungrier than a starvin' boll weevil in a rotten cotton patch. Bring on the eats. It is nice to know the star of the show. Ain't it, now? What do you think, Jesse?"

"I am happy and proud, but I feel a little upstaged by all this excitement," Jesse commented.

"Only for a moment, Jesse," Harlin replied. "She'll be back. Sometimes we have to hold the reins loosely. Let the filly go at her own pace. Let her dance and prance, but knowing when to pull in the reins to tether—now that's the trick."

"That analogy is so deep, Mr. Parsons," Jesse remarked. "I never looked at a relationship like that. You are so correct."

"I know a few things, Jesse," Harlin stated proudly.

"Yes, about trading and training horses, you do," Mrs. Parsons quipped, leaning over and looking at Jesse. "You want to know all about the filly that's soon to perform, come and see me."

"I will, Mrs. Parsons, and that is certain," Jesse assured.

Hank rolled his eyes, nudged Jesse's arm, and whispered, "They don't know nothin,' Jesse. You want the book on Lady, you see me."

Sitting between the Parsons, Jesse smiled, felt secure, felt a part of something bigger than himself. He had just turned a page to a new chapter in his young life. He was content with their acceptance. And he knew he was smitten.

Darkness fell, and the lights of the fairway brightened. Stage lights came on as the music intensified. Ambient murmur faded as carny barkers cried out.

Then, from far off you could hear a train coming. The stage lights began to dim and the train sounded as if it were getting closer, closer. Then someone spoke. "Ladies and gentlemen, please welcome tonight's main event if you would—a grand welcome for Slo' Hand Scottie and The Trainwreck Survivors. Applause went up, a train whistle sounded, and the sound of rushing steam from an engine gave way as a train appeared to pull into the station, and there stood Mr. Slo' Hand Scottie himself. "Wooo! Hooo!" he shouted. WELCOME, TEXARKANA, TEXAS!

The train rumble faded and gave entrance to the band. They roared to life, featuring Slo' Hand Scottie's signature song. Several songs played through and then the lights dimmed again, and a blue hue colored the stage. Eerie music emanated, mist began to cover the stage, and from backstage, a single light projecting from overhead luminated what seemed to be an apparition. An image of someone veiled, floating as it moved ever so slowly to the front of the stage. The song "Long Black Veil" started, and Slo' Hand Scottie began to sing. At the very end of the song, still in veil but now before the audience, the veil was pulled away and there stood Lady Parsons.

Cheers and applause erupted, and Slo' Hand Scottie pointed to Lady and said, "Please meet and greet Ms. Lady Parsons, outstanding performer and winner of this year's Bowie County talent show. Lady, you have the stage!"

"Thank you, folks, for that warmest of welcomes! I want to thank Mr. Slo' Hand Scottie for sharing front and center and providing the great backup band, The Trainwreck Survivors, who are magnificent in their musical endeavors. Thank you, thank you, and thank you!"

"The first song I want to perform is called 'I've Got a Mansion,' and last night here at this park, someone very special to me promised that he would build me a mansion. Thank you, Jesse! And so it goes: 'I've Got a Mansion' followed by 'Country Roads'."

At the end of "Country Roads," as promised, Lady changed a few of the lyrics, mentioning the roads leading home again to the northeast Texas pines. When the song was finished, it seemed that the whole fair exploded—not a person remained in a seat. The crowd rose to the occasion, hooting and hollering in the hope that she might sing more. But Lady declined.

Slo' Hand Scottie kept pointing to Lady. She raised her hand and people calmed and slowly sat back down.

All of a sudden, a young man—it was Jesse—ran to the front of the stage and handed Lady a bouquet of red roses. As soon as they were delivered, he ran back to his seat and confidently folded his arms, sporting a huge grin.

Slo' Hand Scottie pointed at Lady. "No longer a secret—Lady Parsons has got an admirer!"

"I think I have just been upstaged by the person who said he would build me a mansion," Lady faltered as a tear ran down her cheek. "Thank you, Jesse! I'll hold you to it!"

Another round of applause as Lady looked at the Parsons entourage. She asked sheepishly, "Did you guys know?"

Thumbs up from the comfy seats.

She again graciously thanked everyone. "It is possible," she suggested, "that you will see us together again at another show down the road." Lady beamed with a smile and blew a kiss to the front row comfy seats. "And now," Lady shouted out, "Back to Slo' Hand Scottie and The Trainwreck Survivors!"

Backstage, Lady was greeted by her family and friends. Hugs all around and nothing but praises came from their lips.

"And you," Lady said, making her right hand into a pistol, "should be shot, Jesse James! I guess the cat is really out of the bag now. The whole world knows how much you care."

"Nah," Jesse responded humbly, "it was from all of us. Your coming-out gift."

"It was your idea, Jesse," Hank blurted out. "No denying that one."

"Thank you," Lady whispered, "they are beautiful."

Brad Hastings appeared and declared, "This is one talented la … gal right here, folks. And when Scottie gets finished with the show, he wants to talk about some upcoming performances. You heard—the crowd went nuts over that mist and veil thing we did. In the country venue, people ain't never seen this kind of stage theatrics before. We are on the cutting edge of ideas with this—country music-wise. What do you say—wanna pursue this? We got the money if you got the time."

THE BALLAD OF JESSE AND LADY IN TUNE

The phone rang at the James residence and Jesse's father picked up the receiver. "Hello, Chester James here."

"Hi, Mr. James. Lady Parsons speaking. May I talk to Jesse?"

"Yeah …by the way, I saw you on *News Live*. I was impressed! And Jesse, he ain't doin' nothin' but loafing around. That's what he does best. Hold on. Hey, kid, it's that young filly singer from across the hill wantin' ta talk at ya! He'll be right here, my dear."

Jesse took the phone from his dad, "Really, thanks Dad …."

Giving his son a wink, Chester interjected as he whispered, "Hey, no problem. Lookin' good right there, boy. Latch on ta that one and ride it out ta the end. Know what I mean?"

Holding his hand over the phone he gave his dad a look. "Oh, hey there, hi," he greeted.

"Hi yourself." Lady saluted. "So, since you are just loafing around, not doing anything but nothing …you want to meet me at the tree so we can do nothin' together?"

Jesse replied, "I am a bit tired from being too busy loafing to do much else."

"Cool. I'll see ya in less than fifteen."

After hanging up, Jesse headed straight for the back door, hoping to miss his father on the way out. But Chester was sitting at the table having coffee. "Where ya going in such a hurry?" he asked with a smirk. "Guess I already know?"

Jesse didn't answer and headed directly to the oak tree. Lady was waiting with her horse, Silky, tethered to a tree.

Smiling, Lady speculated, "Well look at you. What do you have hidden behind your back? Is it something special for a very special Lady?"

"It just might be," Jesse answered, handing her a plaque with a red rose.

Lady read the inscription. It was Proverbs 16:3 "'Commit thy works unto the LORD, and thy thoughts shall be established.' This is so sweet. And the red rose ...means passion."

"Song of Solomon," Jesse replied, "chapter two, one and two: 'I am the rose of Sharon, and the lily of the valleys. As the lily among the thorns, so is my love among the daughters.' And I must add, my love for you."

"You are so romantic, Jesse. Just like you surprised me at the concert," Lady exclaimed. "This will make me cry. I am overwhelmed."

"No, no, please don't do that ... please," Jesse begged. "Let's sit down and I will show you from the Bible—the Song of Solomon 2:16. 'My beloved is mine, and I am his: he feedeth among the lilies.'"

Leaning on Jesse's shoulder, Lady took his hand and said, "I think that you are, and I am yours."

"Lady, I feel complete when I am with you, and ... you scare me. Like at the concert, I felt like only up there were you complete. I never want to feel the opposite—incomplete." Quickly changing the subject, Jesse continued, "Let's see what the verses say."

Lady responded, "I think I already know. It is about falling in and out of grace. The coming back, the intimacy of humanity. As our sacred commitments to marriage have suffered, we have perverted it by our sin. I want to be sure about my love, Jesse ... don't want it to be made a lie by this world."

"That is so deep—it is what I love about you," Jesse stated.

A smile came across Lady's lips and she asked, "How much do you love me, Jesse?"

"I have gone and done it, haven't I?" Jesse confessed.

"What?"

"Totally made myself vulnerable. I am way too vulnerable."

"I get the point, and I won't hurt you without advance warning," Lady advised and then punched him in the shoulder. "Oops, guess I didn't warn ya, and that's what y'all git if ya do me wrong, right there in your kisser."

"Glad that wasn't my nose," Jesse commented.

The lunch bell at the Parsons' farm began ringing. Jesse added, "Whew, saved by the bell!"

Jumping up, Lady pulled Jesse to his feet. "Come with me, Jesse. We can both ride Silky!" Silky whinnied and shook her head.

"See, Silky shook her head no. Besides, I am on a mission," Jesse pleaded. "Got a new carpenter project going on that needs immediate attention."

"Okay for now, Jesse," Lady agreed. "Carny food was great, but you can't put off coming to my house to break bread with the family forever. Also, I have another show coming up. I want you to come with Hank and me. He's driving me to these gigs." Lady placed the plaque in her saddle bag. In one continuous motion she settled onto the saddle and blew Jesse a kiss. "Soon, Jesse James—very soon." Lady placed the rose in her teeth and turned the horse toward the ranch.

"Vaya con Dios. Te adoro!" Jesse shouted.

As he stood there, again the carny barker's comment came to mind, "And that's some gal you got there." *To be sure*, Jesse pondered, *to be sure*.

Upon entering the garage workshop back at his house, Jesse immediately went to the workbench. There was the guitar he had found in one of the old houses that he and his father were renovating. He picked it up, admiring his handiwork. Yes, the neck was straight, new tuning heads, new strings. He plucked each string and attempted an open E chord. Seems in tune, he said to himself, and added, "I think she is going to like this."

Jesse wrapped up the guitar, placed a beginners' book on how to play the guitar inside an envelope, and began a letter to go along with it. When he finished, he grabbed his Bible and headed for the old oak tree.

Mission complete, Jesse thought, *or has the quest just begun?*

The sun was up, and it was a grand display of a morning; diamonds of dew glistened off the verdant hills of the Parsons ranch. Lady was exhilarated as she placed the saddle and reins on Silky. It was routine to her. She loved her painted pony and had named her for her silk-like mane and tail. Lady gave Silky the greeting of an apple in hand and a huge hug. Talking out loud to the horse, Lady said, "Need to do some serious thinking today, Silky, and some writing in my poetry book. And let's not forget about my diary." Silky snorted in affirmation, as she knew the routine and welcomed it.

"I know it's a little boring for you while I sit and write underneath an old mister shady tree," Lady said. Silky gave a whinny and Lady smiled as she got into the saddle. Going to the shady tree was a common journey for Lady and Silky. They crossed the stream and galloped through the meadow, and just about three-quarters of a mile away from the house stood the old oak tree. Its breadth and location made it different from the rest; its span of branches were massive and it had earned the right to be there. It had stood the test of time.

Lady and Silky were just about at the tree when Silky stopped and snorted. "What's wrong, Silky?" Lady asked. "You see a snake or something? I didn't bring my trusty single-barrel."

As Lady urged Silky forward, she spied what Silky considered foreign. Something was leaning against the tree. It was a package with a large manila envelope attached to it. "Was it a jolly old elf that left this gift?" Lady asked the horse as she got out of the saddle.

Tethering Silky, Lady walked over and removed the envelope from the package and questioned out loud, "Well, what could this be, Silky?"

Upon opening the envelope, she pulled out a *Guitar for Beginners* book and a handwritten letter. Lady proposed, "Obviously what's in the odd-shaped package must be a guitar. But before opening the box let's read the letter. May I read it out loud to you, Silky?"

Silky snorted in approval.

"Thank you, Silky." Lady continued, "Now the handwriting is less than perfect but I shall endeavor to make it out. And it goes on to say, 'Dear Lady'—now that's a good start—'I know that this may sound weird, but I have watched you coming to the tree for a long time now, far longer than you have actually known about me, in fact. One time I saw you slip and fall into the stream when you stopped to give your horse a drink. I wanted to call out and ask if you were okay, but I was afraid, because you might have thought it wrong of me to be hanging around in a tree. I look forward to and have enjoyed our many talks and studies. It was really great that you decided to go with me to the fair because you made me feel really special. And the concert blew me away.' Hmmm, Silky, do you think he's stalking me?"

The horse whinnied and shook her head no.

"Good, because I don't think so, either," Lady agreed and continued reading, "'I am not stalking you or anything like that, and I respect and cherish our relationship.' See, Silky, we were right! 'I found this old guitar in the trash when my dad and I were renovating a house. I cleaned it up, put oil on it to retain the original finish, made sure the neck was straight, put new strings on it, and tried to tune it the best I could. The man at the music store told me the guitar was old but had a great sound and was a rare old piece. I know you write stuff and I've heard you sing, of course. Even when you didn't know I was listening. And at the baptism you sounded amazing. Thought you could put your words to music. You truly are musical. So here it is, I hope you like it. Your bestest friend ever, Jesse. P. S. Hopefully no one else finds it and the critters don't eat it. See ya soon! Love ya, Jesse.'"

Content within herself and the beauty of the day, Lady looked out over the pasture and the surrounding hills. She whispered, "This is just too perfectly sweet."

Taking her book of poetry and the diary from the saddle bag, Lady gave Silky a carrot, sat back down and wrote, *We the finite seek immortality; being the dust of the earth, we are envious of the angels.* Looking at her handwritten page, Lady suddenly felt odd and asked out loud, "Where did that come from? I think we'll head back to the barn." Getting up, she grabbed the still-packaged guitar, placed it in one of the saddle bags, and prepared to ride. A breeze from the hilltop caught her back and gave her a chill. Nervously she turned around and peered up the hill towards Jesse's house.

Approaching the barn, Lady could see Hank unloading a pick-up full of feed for the livestock. He stopped his chore to help her down from the horse. "What's in the package?" he asked.

"It's a guitar that Jesse gave me as a gift," she announced.

"Uh, oh! This sounds ever so serious, Lady," Hank chortled.

Lady responded with, "Right now he is just a great friend of mine and you know it. Besides, this is so thoughtful of him, and he had no clue that I have always wanted a guitar; he just did this out of kindness of heart. And if you want to know, yes, I love him—his thoughts and kindness are never ending. So there you have it."

Hank smiled at his sister's rhetoric and said, "He is all that, isn't he? I like Jesse because you like Jesse. You believe in him and that's the long and short of it. Sit down over there on that hay bale and unwrap it, then. I need to get back to work. While you're at it, gaze over yonder at who has come to call."

Looking past Hank, Lady spied the town know-it-all's Crown Vic parked in front of the ranch house and commented, "Well looky here, old Alma's come to call. She's the one who is always callin' us 'those highfalutin horsey people from Ken-tuck-ee.' But each and every time she's needin' a donation or backup on one of her personal agendas, she shows up pleading empty pockets to Momma."

"Brought along one of her busybodies for backup," Hank stated. "They looked pretty serious, too. I'd like to be a mouse in Momma's apron pocket right now."

"And where's Poppa while all this is goin' on?" Lady asked.

"Where do ya think?" said Hank. "When Poppa saw them pull up, he quickly hopped on the tractor and said something about a fence needed fixin' way over on the other side of the creek. He took his fishing pole along."

Laughing, Lady said, "Smart man, our Poppa. What do you say we do a little fishing over by the open kitchen window?"

Giving a nod and a wink, Hank replied, "The chores can wait a little, with all this necessary fishing going on. Let me put Silky up and I'll catch up to you in a minute."

Arriving at the kitchen window not a moment too soon, Lady tapped into the coffee-and-cake conversation. She could hear Alma's distinguishable voice leading the conversation: "Now understand that you didn't hear it from me, Ms. Parsons, but since she passed on last evening, the boy is going to be sent to live with the mother's brother. They're Okees, live on a five-hundred-acre ranch ... extremely well off. Found oil on their acreage to the tune of hundreds of barrels a week. Nets them over forty thousand dollars a month, I was told. Lucky boy for sure. Can't say much about the old man, though. Gets whatever he deserves, is my way of thinking."

"Surely the boy's father must have something to say about the matter," said Ms. Parsons.

Alma added, "Don't think that old man cares one way or the other. What with the wife and child out of the way, he can go on and do whatever he pleases. Free as a bird, without any obligation except in the end to the good Lord Himself to answer to."

> **"**
> We, as Christian folk, no matter what the problems with Mr. James, need to provide a post-interment gathering. There should be comfort for the grieving and warm food to help everyone feel welcome.
> **"**

Sneaking up on Lady, who was engrossed listening to the unfolding conversation, Hank poked her in the ribs. Almost giving up her position, she turned around. She sternly placed her fingers over her lips. Then, with guitar in hand, she motioned for Hank to follow her. In the meantime, the conversation continued, with Mrs. Parsons speaking up: "We, as Christian folk, no matter what the problems with Mr. James, need to provide a post-interment gathering. There should be comfort for the grieving and warm food to help everyone feel welcome."

Alma's friend Gertrude gently slapped the table and added, "You are so right, Mrs. Parsons, and that is precisely why we are here. Our small church does not have a proper fellowship hall. We thought, perhaps hoped, you could open up your spacious sitting room and kitchen to such an idea."

"This is such a good idea," Alma said as she jumped into the concept. "By doing so, it would go such a long way to introduce your kind and benevolent family to further relations with church and community."

Quickly adding to bring closure, Gertrude asked, "So what do you think? And how can we help?"

"Well, of course we can do a little something here to help make all feel warm and welcome," replied Mrs. Parsons.

"Wonderful, it is done then," declared Alma. While pushing a piece of paper towards Ms. Parsons, she added, "Here is the list of things we will need from you. The viewing is Saturday evening, and the funeral and burial are Sunday morning. Gertrude and I will be here early Sunday morning to help put everything in order."

"It is so wonderful to have you as part of our mission," Gertrude stated.

"You are welcome, ladies," Mrs. Parsons said with a smile.

Smiling back, the two ladies looked approvingly at each other and Alma said, "Gertrude and I will be going now, as we have much to do on our journey today. Please don't get up, Mrs. Parsons, we can surely see our way out. Again, thanks to you and your family."

Mrs. Parsons nodded and smiled as the two ladies exited the kitchen and went out the front door. Through the back door sneaked Lady and Hank, pretending not to have heard a word. Lady had her new guitar in hand. Momma asked, "Well did you two get an earful by the kitchen window?"

"No, not really … what's going on?" Lady asked. "How'd you know we were … ?"

"I get paid to know," Momma stated. "You didn't put two and two together? Those two just roped me into holding a wake here Sunday morning. Failed to see that one coming. And what's that you are holding in your hand … where'd you get it?"

Lady explained with excitement, "Jesse left me this gift by the big oak this morning. You know I said how much …."

Momma put up her hand for silence. "Please, you two have to take a seat. We need to talk about your good friend Jesse. It is obvious you did not pick up on who our conversation was about."

Bewildered, Hank and Lady sat as their mother unpacked the story. "Mrs. James passed away last night. Her husband was out doing whatever it is he does, leaving Jesse alone to look after his mother. Things apparently went from bad to worse as she stopped breathing. Jesse called for the ambulance, but when they arrived they could not bring her around; it was too late."

Hank was silent but clenched his fists. Lady became emotional as she exclaimed, "Oh ... poor Mrs. James ... poor Jesse. We have to go and find him, Hank. He has to be hurting something terrible. He's all alone, Momma."

Holding up her hands for all to calm down, Momma warned, "Hold on now, not so fast. I know you have good intentions, but let's contemplate this."

"I understand, Momma," Lady pleaded. "But Jesse is all alone. If something happened to you and Poppa, heaven forbid ... just like Jesse, Hank and I probably wouldn't know what to do other than call an ambulance. And who knows how long it would take to get here? Just let Hank and me walk over there."

Considering the plea for compassion, Mrs. Parsons took a deep breath and said, "Okay, but here it is. Be smart and cautious when you go over there. If Jesse is by himself, you can bring him back here. You're right to believe that he shouldn't be alone. But if his father is there, you stay away. Are you two hearing me?"

"Loud and clear, Momma," Hank responded.

"Don't go and stick your beaks in someone else's family matter," Momma cautioned. "I don't trust that old man, especially if he's drinking. No telling what frame of mind he's in. Go on now, get over there."

Heading out the back, Hank and Lady quickly walked the mile to the James's property line and stopped short just behind the garage. They saw a screened window at the back of the house. Loud male voices could be heard, and it seemed that a heated conversation was taking place.

"What in the world, Hank ... we have to do something," Lady said frantically.

"Shhh! You heard what Momma said," Hank warned. "Besides, what can we do—ride in there like the Lone Ranger and Tonto to save the day?"

Attempting a plan, Lady suggested, "I'll sneak around the side of the house and politely knock on the front door. I can pretend that I'm taking donations for a school food drive."

Grabbing Lady's arm before she set off, Hank stopped her. "Oh no you don't, Sis. That's clever, but if anyone goes in, it'll be me. At least I can defend myself better than you."

"That's why you're the big brother, big brother," Lady said with a smile. "But we'd better be quick ... sounds like it's gettin' worse."

"You weren't here, dad ... you never were when mom needed you most," Jesse exclaimed. "I always told you to come back soon. You just told me, you're the big man now, be tough, and that you would be back. Well, you never did!"

"Shut your mouth, boy, and don't back sass me," Chester yelled. "You probably gave your poor Momma too much of that pain medicine ... is that what you did, boy, tryin' to off her?"

"Absolutely not, Poppa—you killed her!" Jesse shouted back.

"What did you say boy?" Chester said with a snarl!

"You killed her by breaking her heart. That's what YOU did Poppa, that's what YOU did to us," Jesse yelled, "You left us a long time ago!"

Suddenly there was a crashing noise coming from the house. Hank and Lady could hear physical wrestling as the tussle continued.

Hank looked around for something to carry into battle. "I can't take this, Lady," he said hurriedly as he began to climb the fence.

Grabbing hold of Hank's shoulder, Lady cautioned him, "Hold on just another minute and I'll go with you. There's safety in numbers."

More vitriol flowed through the back window from Jesse, "I hate you, old man ... I hate you with all my soul!"

"That's it boy, now you're showing some spunk," Chester sneered. "Where you going? You'd better get back here, boy! If you leave, you don't come back ... ever! You hearin' me ... never! You can't leave me. You ain't got no place to go!"

They stood like two deer in the headlights. Lady and Hank watched as the back door burst open and it was Jesse who appeared. He ran into the garage and they heard things being moving about. Suddenly they heard him coming, running around the corner and into Hank's arms. He grabbed Jesse in a hug and said, "Hey, hold up, man, what's going on?"

Jesse looked over at Lady ... quickly turning away, hiding tears and a bruised face. Lady softly said, "It's okay Jesse, we're here now. Momma said to bring you back, you are leaving with us. Now. He ain't gonna touch you anymore, I promise."

Indiscriminate ranting could be heard coming from the house. Chester was apparently roaring drunk as he spewed out his vile rhetoric. "You're no better than that sickly old wasp I was married too. I ain't gonna miss any of ya!"

The threesome turned away, leaving the rage and hatred behind them. Arriving once again where their friendship began, at the oak tree, they paused and looked toward the ranch. Lady remembered that it was close to suppertime and Momma did say to bring him back, but she was curious about the box that Jesse was holding.

Noticing Lady's curiosity, Jesse commented, "It's my good-memories box and my Bible. I know you probably think it's silly but they both give me comfort and hope. But hope the Bible does that for me."

"After hearing all that went on back there," Hank commended Jesse, "I believe you to be the bravest person I have ever met. You have put up with more than I could bear."

"Got to take this all in, Jesse," Lady invited, "Let's just sit down for a while."

Sitting down, Jesse was positioned in the middle. He sensed that the Parsons twins took a defensive posture for him. He felt that no more harm would come to him, if the Parsons have anything to say about it.

Speaking up first, Jesse startled the Parsons twins. "It's not his fault, you know."

"Who?" Lady asked.

"My poppa—it's not his fault," Jesse answered.

"Not that you are crazy—but how do you mean it's not his fault?" Hank questioned. "I saw, I heard, and I am here to testify on your battered behalf."

Putting his head in his hands, Jesse spoke, though he was holding back the welling emotion. Jesse somehow felt his father's pain. Lady and Hank put their arms around Jesse, trying to comfort him.

"He's sick, the demon's got him and won't let go. He can't help himself and he's afraid to admit it," Jesse explained. "Thinks he can win the battle all by himself; but not knowing the truth, he can't."

"How do you know all this?" Lady asked.

Presenting his Bible, Jesse answered, "It tells me all about Poppa and his problem, and how to heal it if he would only listen, only hear the message. And Momma, she's resting peaceful now. No more pain, no more broken heart, and I will see her again soon, that's for certain."

"Wow, Jesse," Hank said, "you've grasped hold of the faith, my friend. What is in your good box of memories?"

Opening it, Jesse smiled as he shuffled through the contents and pulled out a roll of photos. "The good-memories box has photos of you and me, Lady!"

"Ooowee," Hank pretended to be stunned. He cajoled, "So that's where you two snuck off to, holding hands all the while. Can't fool me—and wait 'til Momma finds out!"

"Really, Hank—until Momma finds out. You always threaten me with that—so juveee," Lady retorted. "Thanks to your big mouth, Momma already knows, but I don't think she cares at this point. Don't worry Jesse, we're on the same team."

Laughing now, Jesse felt the tension begin to fade as he pulled out a few more photos. "Here's one of my family back when Momma wasn't sick and Dad wasn't drinking. This was taken on my uncle's ranch. That's me on the horse. They were trying to teach me how to ride that day."

"How did you do?" Lady asked.

"I guess okay," Jesse replied. "Never got a chance to keep practicing."

"We'll give you that chance, won't we Hank?" Lady affirmed.

"You can count on it, pard," Hank agreed. He saw an envelope Jesse was holding and asked, "What's in your hand?"

"It's a letter my momma said to keep safe and away from Poppa until she died," Jesse explained. "I guess now is the time. I have no idea what it means or says. There's a lot of legal stuff and it seems like mumbo jumbo to me. It's a will, I guess."

"We'll let Poppa have a look," Lady suggested. "He'll know what to do."

"I think we know what to do right now," Hank said, observing the ranch house. "Momma's out on the porch looking this way. I believe she's waving the dish towel and the bell will soon begin to ring. That means we'd better get there before she feeds the dogs."

HOME AT THE PARSONS

Upon entering the kitchen, the three noted that Mrs. Parsons was busy preparing to set food on the table. Poppa was seated at the head of the table in hope of what was about to be served. Jesse looked about and noticed how everything was in order and this made him feel very comfortable. Hank was the first to introduce the circumstances. "We found him, Momma, a little worse for wear, but he's gonna be okay." Pausing, Hank's nose caught a familiar aroma, "Having fish tonight?" he asked

Poppa gave a thumbs-up and sported a big smile.

Turning away from the stove, Momma greeted Jesse and offered him her hand. Poppa got up from the table and came over to greet him. "Welcome to our home again, Jesse."

"We are sorry for your loss," Momma said, adding, "You are welcome to stay here as long as you need."

"My sentiments as well, Jesse, said Poppa. I can't begin to imagine what you have gone through. Let me affirm what Momma just said; you are welcome here. Let me take your things and set them on the counter for now; they seem important to you."

"Yes sir, thank you, sir," Jesse replied. Poppa smiled at his respectfulness.

"Hank, Lady," Momma commanded, "Show Jesse the ropes around here on the ranch. Wash up before we break bread and be quick about it."

Hank whispered to Jesse, "Let's go to the mud room." Jesse got a funny look on his face but reluctantly followed along. When they got back to the table, everything was ready. They all seated themselves and Jesse bowed his head and began to pray silently. Respectfully, they all waited for him to finish.

"You may share if you want to, Jesse," Momma said.

"I don't want to pressure anyone. I always pray silently," Jesse replied.

"You don't have to worry about that in this house," Poppa said, trying to put Jesse at ease. "We will invite you to please pray out loud and include us as well. I certainly don't mind having a few words spoken to the good Lord on my behalf."

"Thank you, sir, I will next time, and I did include all of you," Jesse said with a smile.

"Yes, include me, Jesse," Hank said. "With all my evil thoughts Lord knows I need praying for."

"Don't make fun, Hank," Lady scolded. "But he's right, Jesse. All those nasty pranks Hank pulled on me—especially your infamous burning poo bag ploy."

"What in the world is a poo bag?" Hank asked innocently.

"If you happen to see a burning paper bag somewhere on the farm," Lady explained, "please don't stomp on it to put it out. Throw water on it, or better yet, call for Hank—he'll be close by—and ask him to get rid of it."

"Oh, I get it, a poo bag of the horse variety," Jesse surmised.

"Yup, that's the one," Lady said with a smile, and added, "And a very fresh one, I might add."

Everyone at the table laughed out loud at Lady's expense, of being suckered into the poo bag ploy.

The frivolity was cut short as Momma warned, "All right, that is not decent table talk; enough about the poo."

Taking Momma's strong hint, Poppa changed the subject. "How are you holding up, Jesse? This is some ordeal for a young man to be going through."

"Oh, I am okay with it, sir," Jesse replied, trying to be positive. "Momma was seriously ill for a very long time and I watched her suffer. But now the pain is over and she is at peace. I am certain that this is for the best."

"That is so mature that you see it that way, Jesse," Poppa said. "Good for you, because many would see this and try to cast blame on someone or something."

"Poppa, Jesse has something that looks very important that he needs someone to look at," Lady said. "His momma gave it to him before she passed."

"Well, it must be in that box you are carrying, because your wardrobe can't fit in there," Mr. Parsons said, trying to lighten the moment. "Unless of course, Jesse, you feel it too personal to share?"

"Oh no, sir, I trust you completely," Jesse stated.

"Hank, hand Jesse the box," Lady suggested. "Poppa, I think you'll know what it is and be able to advise him what to do."

Jesse opened it, took out the envelope, and placed it in Mr. Parsons' hand. "Here ya go, sir. It is from an attorney who made this for my mother. I was told that this concerns me and my future. Momma said that my father shouldn't see this, so that's why I hid it and never told anyone until now."

"Smart lad," Poppa remarked as he opened the envelope and began to read it to himself. He asked, "Jesse, do you have any idea what this letter contains?"

"I gather from looking over it that it might be a will," Jesse answered.

"I say again—smart lad." Mr. Parsons continued, "This is your mother's last request. It was signed and sealed over two years ago. She must have known then how serious her affliction was."

"What does it say, Harlin?" Mrs. Parsons asked.

"Yes, Poppa, tell Jesse so he knows," Lady prodded.

Everyone put down their utensils in the hope of hearing a revelation, and Harlin made it concise. "First of all, the attorney who composed this—I know him, as well, and I am sure he will be looking you up to make this all official. So I will tell you succinctly that your mother gave you everything that belonged to her on this earth. It appears that you will be well taken care of, son. That's it in a nutshell. All the figures and numbers are best left to you and your attorney. You should, or if you want me to, I'll call him in the morning. We need to let him know where you are."

There was silence as everyone waited for Jesse to answer. But he was holding back an oncoming wave of emotion as best he could. Shaking his head, Jesse was about to burst until Hank slapped his back and uttered, "Woo–eee, buddy! I like you now more than ever! Now that is good news! Of course I feel bad and all, but hearing this puts me at ease. 'Cause I know for sure when you and my sister get hitched, you are going to be able to take care of her in the fashion that she deserves!" Hank grabbed Jesse and gave him a hug.

"Hank!" Lady exclaimed.

"Stop this, both of you!" Momma commanded. "I sorta know why you did that, Hank, but what you said is inappropriate at this time."

"You are correct, Momma," Harlin agreed. "Hank, that was a little out of line and we should move on once Jesse grabs some composure. We hope that Jesse realizes that we are not all as crazy as you, Hank."

"No sir, Mr. Parsons," Jesse replied. "Hearing about the poo bag ... and now Hank's insane ranting about Lady and me. I couldn't agree with you more, that he is certifiably crazy." Jesse looked at Hank with a smile.

Everyone had a good laugh and Momma made another suggestion. She asked loudly, "Dessert, anyone? There is a watermelon hiding out in the ice box and coconut custard pie on the sideboard. You may have one or the other, or if you are feeling adventurous, you might have both."

Hearing and accepting the call, crazy Hank jumped to the forefront of the action. Mr. Parsons rolled his eyes and shook his head as Hank jumped up to give an oratory, attempting a nasally English accent: "I am on the hunt, Chief Parsons, for the culprit. We have placed the murdered melon on ice and are on the hunt for who we believe to be the villain—that being mean Mr. Custard."

Attempting to stop Hank's shenanigans, Mr. Parsons held up his hand. "Okay, Sherlock, go get those arrested or murdered and bring them before the jury so we may all share in their just desserts."

Jesse got up and said, "Hey, I will help bring those accused to the table, as well. Hank can't have all the fun."

"I think we're all gonna be just fine," Momma stated. "What do you think, Lady?"

Smiling in agreement, Lady nodded and said, "I feel so good about Jesse, Momma, and how he ... fits into the family and I ...."

Just then Lady was cut off by the sound of an approaching vehicle. It was speeding up in the driveway and then it spun around in front of the house, sending stones and dust everywhere; some ended up on the front porch.

"It's my dad," Jesse said. "I recognize the sound of his pick-up truck. Man, I am so sorry to bring this to your home."

"Not your fault, Jesse," Harlin replied. "Everyone stay put, and I mean right where you are, and that means you, too, Jesse. Your father has rights but not in his drunken condition, and right now he's trespassing on Parsons' property. Harlin motioned to his wife. "The phone, Momma—the sheriff!" She affirmed with a nod and picked up the receiver and started dialing.

Jesse had sat down but now made a motion to get up. Lady grabbed him, not letting him move, and she spoke into his ear, "Oh, no you don't, Jesse dear. I told you no harm would come to you. I keep my promises."

Looking longingly into Lady's eyes, Jesse smiled an honest smile. From this day forward, he would remember how good it felt and how he trusted Lady to hold his heart in her hand.

> **"**
> From this day forward, he would remember how good it felt and how he trusted Lady to hold his heart in her hand.
> **"**

Mr. Parsons turned around just in time to see Jesse's transformation from friend to confidant in his daughter and said protectively, "Jesse, your dad does not know you are here. But that's a card I am not willing to turn. It will buy us time until the sheriff arrives."

As the drama unfolded, Momma's voice could be heard in conversation with the sheriff. "Yes, we got a situation out here on the ranch and it's about to turn ugly. Chester James is out here drunk as a February skunk in heat. He's thinkin' his son is over here and thinkin' to do no one any good, as I see it. You need to head on over here, and now!" Momma hung up the phone and smiled, "Sheriff's a-comin'!"

"Good—good," Harlin said. "All we gotta do is hold Chester at bay and buy a little time."

The slamming of the truck door could be heard, and it appeared that Chester was stirring himself up a little courage as he bellowed out, "BOY! YOU IN THERE HOLDIN' UP WITH THE HORSEY PEOPLE ... TRYIN TO TAG THAT PRETTY YOUNG FILLY, AREN'T YA? TAKIN' AFTA THE OLD MAN'S MY GUESS! IF YOU ARE IN THERE ... YOU BETTER ANSWER ME, BOY, OR I'M A GONNA HAVE TA TAKE ACTION—YOU HEARIN' ME?"

Harlin walked over to the screen door and stood to one side. Peering out, he saw Chester leaning against the pick-up and said, "Why, Chester, is that you? I hardly would know ya."

"What the heck you asking, is it me?" Chester responded with slurred speech. "Of course it's me, Harlin. Who do you think it is—Santy Claus—you hiding my boy in there?"

"As I said, I hardly recognize you, Chester," Harlin replied. "What have you been doing with yourself?"

"Well, that's a pretty dumb question, ain't it, Harlin?" Chester questioned. "Bein' that my wife just died and now my boy's run off."

"Sorry hearing about your wife, Chester. That's too bad," Harlin answered, trying to keep the brakes on, "and I know you're surely gonna miss her."

"Why don't you come out on the porch where I can see ya, Harlin?" Chester asked.

"Seeing just fine from where I'm at Chester," Harlin replied, and asked, "What did you say you were needin' again?"

Shuffling around now and walking back and forth Harlin could see that Chester was becoming frustrated with the roadblock that was being thrown in his path.

"Oh come on now Harlin, quit stalling," Chester said now raising his voice. "IT'S MY BOY I WANT. I KNOW HE'S IN THERE! HE'S MY CONCERN—NOT YOURS! DON'T MAKE ME COME IN THERE AND FETCH 'EM!"

Turning his head, Chester saw lights reflecting off the hood of his truck. The sheriff's car and a tow truck were coming up the driveway.

Chester reacted. "Ah, Harlin, what did you have to go and do that to me? I wasn't gonna start a fight or nothin'. I am sorry. I just want my boy back."

"Not tonight, Chester," Harlin answered. "You need to think on this and sober up. Maybe tomorrow we can discuss things, if you want to."

Flashing lights reflected everywhere in the dark fall night now. And especially through the window where Jesse sadly watched the sheriff handcuff his father and place him in the back seat of the patrol car for safe keeping. Tears formed once again. It had been a long and emotionally tiring day for him. Lady hung on to Jesse and wrapped her arms around him from behind. Jesse clasped her hands that were locked about his chest. Lady whispered again into his ear, "It's going to be okay—you are going to be okay."

Asking the million-dollar question, Jesse whispered back, "Will we be okay, Lady ... us, will we survive?"

"That's a promise," Lady whispered. "Didn't I tell you that when we left your house, we left all that hatred behind?"

"Yes, you did," Jesse affirmed. "And I am holding you to it." Jesse swore that he felt a gentle kiss on his ear from Lady. It made him feel different all of a sudden; time stopped and nothing else in the world mattered. Jesse believed that nothing bad could ever touch him, now or ever again.

With everything secure—Chester locked in the back seat and the tow truck hitching on to the pick-up truck—the sheriff came up the front steps and onto the porch. He asked, "Mr. Parsons, do you want to file charges—harassment, trespassing, unlawful attempt, or anything?"

Mr. Parsons shook his head no and the sheriff answered, "Nope, I didn't think so."

Releasing Jesse, Lady ran her hand across his back. The sheriff looked over at Jesse, smiled, and shook his head. Sheriff Harris spoke up, "Yup, I knew you were in here, son. Harlin, you can make the call in the morning as to how you want to proceed. I heard from the neighbors—there was a ruckus going on and that Chester laid hands on the boy, so child abuse is a factor. I am observant enough and I do see marks on Jesse's face. It's how far you want to take it, son, and I am sure you got the witnesses. I'll not belabor the issue now, but do come 'round and contact me in the morning. Okay, Harlin—okay, Jesse?"

"I'll make sure we get in touch, Sheriff," Mr. Parsons assured him. "We have many stops to make tomorrow on Jesse's behalf and you will be one of them."

Mrs. Parsons now came over and said, "I want to thank you, Sheriff Harris, for being so prompt, because we were running out of excuses."

"No, Mrs. Parsons, it is I who needs to thank you for keeping it peaceful until I got here," Sheriff Harris said. "These domestic things can go sideways in a hurry when alcohol content is high and reason goes out the window. See you folks tomorrow."

Finding his way out the front door, Sheriff Harris gave a wave goodbye. Mr. Parsons turned to everyone while wringing his hands and exclaiming, "Whew! I am so glad that's over!" Then he said, "Hank! Where is that murdered melon and the evil Mr. Custard?"

A knock at the door startled Jesse. A familiar voice let Jesse know that it was time to get up. He thought he was dreaming. He believed that he was back at his house and the gentle voice was a dream, but it was quite the opposite. Last evening's events unwound like a newsreel. As he looked around, Jesse's heart skipped a beat. Unfamiliar pictures decorated the walls. Relatives from a bygone era—but they were not his relatives. Several military uniforms all neatly pressed and on display hung from several points in the room, along with the faces to whom they belonged. Jesse wondered, didn't anyone ever smile back in the day? Then his nose caught the smell of home cooking. There was a pile of clean clothes at the foot of the bed and a robe hung on the door hook. On the nightstand was a note:

> Wake up sleepyhead! You were out like a light and huffing like a coal train going up a grade. Don't blame you for snoozing. You've been through too much. Robe on the hook, bathroom to the left, some of Hank's clothes that I think will fit you, and breakfast is waiting. Daylight's burning. See ya! Your pal, Lady Jane Parsons—oops! Now I've gone and done it ... revealed myself—my middle name.

Making it gracefully through the morning routine, Jesse made his way down the steps to the kitchen. They were all there at the table. Harlin engrossed in the newspaper, Dot sipping tea, reading a morning devotional, Hank fueling up, and his best friend Lady, now Lady Jane, watching him amble down the steps.

"Good morning, sport," Hank said between bites.

Everyone followed with greetings and Mrs. Parsons said, "Sit down, come and eat before all the vultures finish it up!"

Lady invited, "Sit here by me and I will make sure you are properly fed."

Jesse took a seat. He smelled the enticing aroma of the food. But there was something new added to his morning meal—the scent of a woman. The closeness of this caused him to falter and he dropped a fork on the floor. Dot retrieved it and handed him another. "Are you okay?" she asked.

"Unfamiliar surroundings," Jesse said. "Not used to a morning breakfast prepared and set before me." He added, "Beautiful company to share this with. Thank you."

"Beautiful company—of course he is talking about me," Lady stated confidently.

Poppa looked over the top of the newspaper. "A little proud of yourself this morning, Lady?"

"Confident, Poppa, is all," Lady insisted.

"Well, Jesse, when you are up to it, we will head into town and take care of business this morning," Poppa stated.

"Yes, sir, as planned," Jesse affirmed.

"Homeschooling can't wait, Lady ... Hank," Momma instructed. "Jesse has leave because of the unfortunate event. But you two don't have that indulgence. Besides, we must prepare for the upcoming gathering here at the house come Sunday morning."

"Thank you for doing that, Mrs. Parsons," Jesse said. "I know it will place an inconvenient burden on you folks, but ...."

"Don't worry yourself, young man," Poppa said calmly. "It was an unfortunate event, and we are glad to be able to help. Let's get your life in order. You know you can stay here. We can stop by your house if there is anything you think you might need."

"Yeah, we should stop by there," Jesse said. "I hope my dad's not there."

"We will stop by Sheriff Harris's office first, just to make sure as to what we can or can't do," Mr. Parsons advised. "If you are ready, let's go."

Reaching over, Lady squeezed Jesse's hand, "See ya when you get back."

Getting into the suburban with Mr. Parsons had Jesse a little nervous. Yes, he trusted the man, but he was sure Mr. Parsons might have some questions concerning his intentions with Lady. Rightly so, he thought; justifiable questions, of course.

"So, Jesse," Mr. Parsons began, "I understand that you will be moving to Oklahoma—but not too far away—probably not more than an hour or so. Within driving distance, for sure. All you would need is a good-running inexpensive car to make the trip to see us. You know we would love to see you, and often as you like." Mr. Parsons smiled, looking sideways at Jesse, waiting for a response. Pressing on, Mr. Parsons added, "I know that Lady would love to see you as often as possible, what do you think?"

"Why yes, me too," Jesse agreed. "But Lady is building a career, and from what I can tell she will be traveling, and I believe that is her first love—I mean priority."

"And you are not?" Mr. Parsons asked. "From what I can see, she thinks a lot of you and I would say what I sense is that she might be, dare I say, in love with you?"

"Wow," Jesse said nervously, "you are really putting me on the spot."

"Hey, easy, Jesse," Mr. Parsons added gently. "This is just guys talking, you know, man to man. Let's be honest—Lady is one very attractive and talented girl. And from what I see, you are an honest, kindhearted lad, with honorable and admirable qualities. I could not be more pleased to have my daughter associate with you. The field is open to you, Jesse. Her mother and I talked about it, and you have our blessing."

"I am stunned, Mr. Parsons." Almost becoming emotional, Jesse continued, "So much has happened these last few weeks. It is true, Lady and I have been seeing more and more of each other. And I think that there is now more than friendship between us. She said she would bust my jaw if I betrayed her … so that being said, I think the feeling is mutual … ah, not to break one's jaw … but that we do love each other."

Laughing, Mr. Parsons responded, "Of course not to do physical harm if jilted …. But I get the point. Sounds just like something Lady would demand."

They both laughed at that as they pulled into the sheriff's office. "Good morning," was the Sheriff's greeting. "How was your night, young man, sleeping in unfamiliar surroundings? Not to be smug, but I am sure, better than your dad's cooling off time. He is still locked up at the moment. I can hold him for up to forty-eight hours because of alleged abuse, possible endangerment, unlawful trespass, and even nuisance complaints that were filed by the neighbors. He apparently went into a rage after you left, Jesse. He threw trash and bottles at the neighbors, and actually threatened the people who live next door. So unfortunately, he has made a mess of things."

Again, Jesse became a little emotional. "I know, Sheriff, that he is not the best of men now. But it is sad knowing what he was like before he became demonized by alcohol. He was once a good man. I forgive him, Sheriff … Mr. Parsons. Yet I know he can't come back until he hits bottom, actually remits what is due, and becomes penitent. And I know we can't

> "He was once a good man. I forgive him, Sheriff."

take the risk to see if this is bottom. And by whose standards should that be determined—mine? Certainly not."

"Son, you have blown me away," Sheriff Harris stated. "I understand that you are staying with the Parsons right now. Your momma's funeral is coming up. The wake is at the Parsons' ranch. I will attend, by the way. Jesse, your aunt and uncle are on their way. I am also understanding that you will be headed along back with them. There appears to be no contest from your father with regard to those wishes, I was told."

"Would it be okay if we stop by the James residence so that Jesse can pick up a few of his things that he will be needing?" Mr. Parsons asked the sheriff.

"Of course. In fact, I will follow you over there, fellas. Just to see things proper," Sheriff Harris obliged.

After Jesse grabbed a few things from the house, he and Mr. Parsons went to see the attorney. Mr. Parsons wanted to make sure that what they were proposing to do for the next few days was legal.

Attorney Jenkins was open to answering any and all questions. Jesse handed over the envelope that his mother had given him. Jenkins looked it over and produced a matching copy.

"You understand, Jesse, that you are of legal age to determine for yourself as to where you want to live," stated Attorney Jenkins. "There are requirements for learning curriculum, finishing what is required by law, etc. In your mother's will she strongly suggested you move to the home of Will and Edith Hodges, who live near Idabel, Oklahoma. I am instructed to place into the trust that your mother set up for you, her property near Broken Bow, situated up in the mountain there, all money from her policy, bank accounts, stocks … less, transfer fees, attorney fees, and interment costs. She has designated your Uncle Will and Aunt Edith—whom she trusted—along with me, to be overseers of this trust until you are twenty-one years of age. This is only a short time Jesse—less than four years from now."

Jesse was very quiet and then he asked, "May I have a weekly allowance?"

Both Harlin and Jenkins broke out laughing. Jenkins was the first to speak, "Absolutely, son," he said. "In fact, I have opened an account for you at the bank here in town. It has your name on it and has money in it as well. Your dear mother has allowed you to take out at this time $500 a month until you graduate high school—a stipulated requirement. After that it goes to $1,000 per month. When you hit twenty-one ... well, the trust is all yours to do as you see fit."

Mr. Parsons spoke up. "Jesse, I suggest you keep this all under your hat. I will not broadcast this to anyone. I promise you that. And Attorney Jenkins was kind enough to allow me to be a witness to all this today, as there is client-attorney privilege. We are all good here, Jesse."

Again, Jesse was quiet. "What about my dad?" he asked. "Could he cause something to go wrong with any of this?"

"Your mother's side of the family is a very historical one," explained the attorney. "You're part of a mix of Native American and enslaved African American. Your mother's family received from the US Government land grants. Being part Native also got her a certain stipend. She was a shrewd businesswoman, if you didn't know. She transformed what she had into, well, a small fortune. All she had, she made sure that there would be no contest from anyone, anywhere. What was hers would remain hers, and upon her passing, it now becomes yours and no one else's—no contest. No grievances can come from your father, if that is your concern. God bless the child who's got his own, and that be you, Jesse."

"Wow," was all Jesse could say. "I had no idea—Mom never talked much about it. Kept all this to herself. And of course, Dad never said anything about that side of the family that I can remember."

"Your uncle and aunt, I am sure, can fill in the blanks," Attorney Jenkins assured. "The spread they live on was part of those US grants from back in the day. They managed to hang on to it while many did not." Then the attorney stood up and stated, "That's everything," and he handed Jesse an envelope. "It is all in here, Jesse. Just sign this paper that you received, and you can take it along and review it at your leisure. I am here for you, so if you have any questions, feel free to call or stop by."

On the way back to the ranch, not much was said. Then Jesse spoke up. "What a difference a day makes. Momma never said a word about any of this."

"Apparently there was more to the woman you called momma," Mr. Parsons said.

"Yes, Mr. Parsons, that is now apparent," agreed Jesse. "Hank was right when he slapped me on the back and said, 'Now I can be assured that Jesse can afford to keep Lady as required.'" He chuckled at his recall.

"Never a question on my part," Mr. Parsons said. "And you have earned the right to call me Harlin."

"Okay, Mr. Parsons," Jesse said. "Harlin it is."

"Agreed?" Harlin asked.

"Agreed," said Jesse and they shook on it.

Pulling up in front of the ranch house, Harlin and Jesse noted activity. Hank and Lady were busy setting up two large canopies. Mrs. Parsons, front and center, was doing what she did best—giving instruction on ways and means.

"Hello, darlin', what's going on?" Harlin asked.

"I tossed and turned over this gathering we will be hosting on Sunday," Mrs. Parsons lamented. "It is supposed to be pleasant weather and I thought to keep the pleasantness outside rather than in our parlor. I had Lady and Hank run inta' town and pick up all the necessaries to do just that."

"How can I help?" asked Jesse.

"You and Harlin can set up the folding tables and chairs and set up an area for serving," Mrs. Parsons directed. "I will have the warmers on those tables, as well as drinks and sandwich trays, along with plates, utensils, napkins, and drink containers. We'll prepare what we can and put a tablecloth over the things that need it."

Without muss or fuss, everything got set up and readied for the Sunday wake. Mrs. Parsons stood back and was pleased. "Well done,". she commended. "Take the rest of the day off. Sorry, Harlin; oh, the chores."

Seizing the opportunity, Lady grabbed Jesse by the shirt. "Come on, sport. As promised, we are going to ride some."

Laughing, Hank cautioned, "I don't know, Lady ... he seems like a tenderfoot. Go easy, give him the old mare."

"The old mare," Jesse asked, "Is she gentle ... easy to ride?"

"Yes, don't worry, Jesse," Harlin said. Then he advised, "You guys, don't give him Cherokee. That would be Hank's deal—I am sure that trickster might try to slip a poor unsuspecting rider a gallop on Cherokee. I say don't fall for that one. Cherokee is an all-black quarter horse—can't miss him."

"Thanks for the heads-up," Jesse replied, looking at Hank with suspicion.

Hank shrugged his shoulders and said, "Hey, just tryin' to help is all. Cherokee's a lot of fun, full of spunk, and can jump a rail or two."

"Come on, Jesse," Lady urged, shaking her head. "I wouldn't have let that happen. Sometimes good ol' Hank can be Hanky pranky."

"Hey, I heard that, Sis!" Hank called out.

"Too bad. Sometimes it's true," Lady shouted back and continued, "We'll saddle up Silky and the old gray mare, 'cause like they say, she ain't what she used to be. She's gentle and faithful and watches where she steps—that is important. When she gets tired and wants to go back to the barn, she stops and will go no further. So we will go her distance and come home—sound good?"

"Okay," Jesse replied, "you lead, of course, and I follow. I got it."

Once saddled and on horseback, Jesse saw that Lady had a blanket and a picnic basket. "Are we going on a picnic?" he inquired.

"Good observation," Lady said as she turned and smiled and placed a white cowgirl-looking hat on her head. "Now I am complete. Here ya go—might as well fit the part." She handed a black cowboy hat to Jesse. "It's Hank's—he won't mind."

Lady continued, "Let's pick up the pace just a bit. We will try to make it, if the mare lasts, to Poppa's fishing spot."

The old gray mare went the distance. Lady got down and she steadied Jesse as he came out of the saddle. He said, "Thank you, that was really cool—even crossing the stream was fun."

"See, I told ya," Lady said. "It is fun, isn't it, and no worries … just like the ferris wheel, once you get over yourself and allow things to happen … it's just a matter of time …." Silky nudged Lady into Jesse's arms.

"Now what?" Jesse asked.

"Let's put my blanket on the ground," Lady whispered.

"Then what?"

Lady just smiled and pulled down on the brim of Jesse's hat. "Get over yourself …."

On the ride back to the barn, they took their time. When they came to the stream, they stopped before crossing. Lady asked, "Do you think you are over yourself now?"

"Way over my head," Jesse replied with a smile. "How about you?"

Lady reached for Jesse's hand, held it, and turned to face him. "Like being in this water, totally submerged. I am immersed for the first time, Jesse, in awe of you."

Jesse nodded, smiled, knowing that he had just won the 'Lady lotto.' "For sure," he replied, and urged the old gray mare into the water first. Lady and Silky followed.

"Hey, wait up there, pard," Lady called. For the first time, she discovered someone else who had an edge. She was content with that. Now she knew who Jesse was and how she perceived him in her life.

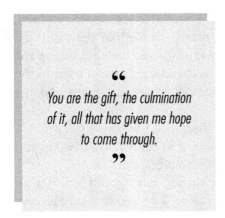

> *You are the gift, the culmination of it, all that has given me hope to come through.*

"These past few weeks have been a never-before time in my life, Lady," Jesse explained. "By and through all the hurt and pain, I have been molded into what I can define as a man within myself. I didn't think it was there, Lady, until now. You are the gift, the culmination of it, all that has given me hope to come through. Don't get me wrong—I thank the Lord for sending me an angel ..." he almost choked on his words ... "that being you."

She stopped, got down from her horse, and demanded, "You get down off that horse and right now."

Quickly Jesse swung his leg over the saddle without thinking and landed straight upright, like a pro rider. "Now what?" he asked.

"And I hope Poppa is watching us," Lady said. She threw off his hat, tossed hers onto the ground, grabbed him, and gave him a passionate kiss. Then she pulled back and stated, "There, I have exposed myself. I have released my inner self to vulnerability, as you say. And Jesse ... what has happened between us today stays between us. I love you completely to the core, and if you ...."

"You will bust my jaw," Jesse finished her sentence.

"Let's get back before they send a search party," Lady said, picking up their hats. Suddenly the dinner bell started ringing in the distance. "You can hear that thing from Never-land," Jesse remarked.

"That's the idea," Lady replied. "And you can be sure that Momma will have her radar on, and antenna tuned in to us, so be cool, dude."

"Well, we weren't drinking or nuthin'," Jesse stated.

"Yeah, well, we been gone most of the afternoon, doing a whole lotta nuthin'," Lady observed.

"Fishin's something. I made homemade rods out of willow branches and used tiny itty-bitty vines and fashioned fishhooks, caught us some nightcrawlers as bait and ..." Jesse rambled.

"And Momma will see through all your verbal drivel and will come up with the answer ... nope, you just keep your beak closed and let me handle it—nod and smile when appropriate. Be your good Jesse self, okay ... okay?"

"Yes, ma'am," Jesse answered and saluted "But ..."

"No buts about it, Jesse ... whew," Lady stated, feeling a little flushed.

Poppa and Hank were returning from the barn when they came upon Lady and Jesse. Hank was the first to speak. "Must have been quite the ride," he said, checking the freckles on his make-believe wristwatch. "It's already supper time."

"And I am hungry guys. Don't know about you, but the dinner bells have been ringing and my stomach's answering," Poppa said. "Put up the horses and let's go eat; we will talk about everything else later."

Food was served and passed around. Jesse said grace and then nobody said anything because their mouths were full of Mrs. Parsons' home cooking. But at last it was Hank who brought up the first table conversation. "So how did she ride, Jesse?"

"What?" Jesse asked sheepishly.

"Old gray mare," Hank clarified with a smirk. "How did she ride?"

"Oh, definitely not a Cherokee," Jesse answered. "Gentle and smooth, no worries there. I just followed the leader."

"You two were gone a long time. Where'd ya go?" Mrs. Parsons asked.

Lady jumped in, "Poppa's getaway retreat—the fishin' hole."

"Oh, do any fishin'?" Poppa asked. "Didn't take any poles with ya—just a blanket and a picnic basket, from what I saw."

"I like fishin,' too, Mr. Parsons," Jesse stated. "I usually take my equipment wherever I go."

Feeling a light kick on his foot, Jesse remembered what Lady said.

"So you fish, do you, Jesse?" Mr. Parsons asked. "We might go back there in a few days. As you tasted the other night, there's some good eatin' swimming around over there."

Jumping back into the conversation, Lady said, "Yes, Jesse was sorta upset because he didn't bring his fishin' gear. He didn't know I was taking him there. He was funny trying to make a rod out of a willow stick and tried to fashion a fishing line out of some vines. Then he whittled a hook out of some bodark wood. While he was doing that, he asked me to find him some bait.

"That's a pretty interesting day you had there," Poppa noted. "Survival skills, huh, Jesse? Did your girl ever find any worthwhile bait?"

"Nothing worthwhile that would catch any fish, sir," Jesse replied.

"It was a good day," Lady said. "We had lunch and talked about what the future might hold, now that Jesse's pretty much on his own. But I assured him that we are here for him. Right, Parsons family?"

"Absolutely, Jesse," Mrs. Parsons replied. "You are part of our family now, right, Harlin?"

"Yes, you are, Jesse," Mr. Parsons agreed.

As the table was cleared, Hank went over to Jesse. "She swam y'all out of that one, pard. I know my sis and whatever you guys were up to, I want you to know is fine by me. I like you like a brother, Jesse—make no mistake about it. Don't cross her, is all I have to say."

"You have my word, and it is a bond," Jesse said, offering Hank his hand.

"Cool," said Hank. "Let's go shoot some darts shooter man, maybe you can teach me some things."

The second Jesse hesitated, Hank laughed out loud, "Sis! You are something else!"

Sunday came. Morning had broken, giving way to mild temperatures and sunshine. A day that all would remember. Just after an early-morning breakfast and instruction from Momma, a car came up the drive. It had Oklahoma plates. There was a knock on the door. Mr. Parsons answered the call. He had been expecting a visit from Oklahomans, but wasn't certain when that meeting would happen.

Upon opening the door ... it was now. "May I help you?" asked Mr. Parsons.

"Yes, hello," was the polite greeting from a tall, well-dressed black man. "We are William and Edith Hodges. Jesse's relatives, aunt and uncle, that is. Ida was my sister. Is this where Jesse is staying?"

"Why yes, of course ... do come in, you are very welcome." Mr. Parsons held out his hand. "I am Harlin Parsons. Dorothy, come here, darlin'," Harlin called out. "It's Jesse's aunt and uncle from Oklahoma come to call."

Mrs. Parsons made her way to the parlor. "It is wonderful to meet at last. I am Dorothy Parsons. Everyone calls me Dot," she stated and offered her hand. "Please come in and sit down, if Harlin hasn't already offered you a seat. Would y'all like some tea and biscuits? They are fresh, as we just finished up breakfast."

"Thank you ... very kind, Mrs. Parsons, but we had breakfast on the way over," Mr. Hodges said. "We just stopped to say hello to Jesse. Get, so to speak. Haven't seen him in years. We were very close for a long time with Ida and her family, but things went in a very wrong direction. With Chester's drinking and all ... he refused to see us. It broke our hearts. Jesse was the only child we had relation to. As we can't have children of our own."

"I see," said Mrs. Parsons. "The boys, that is Hank and Jesse, are doin' the morning chores and should be coming in anytime now."

Jesse is a good boy, no ... let me rephrase," stated Harlin, "a fine young man. One to be proud of, Mr. Hodges."

Mr. and Mrs. Hodges smiled at that. Mrs. Hodges said, "We thought that he might come home with us when this is all over with, the funeral and interment that is. We will be staying around for a few days and hope to, as William said, get reacquainted."

Coming into the room, Lady looked at the Hodgeses and got a strange feeling. One of trepidation and uncertainty.

"This is our daughter, Lady," Harlin introduced. "She is actually Jesse's very best friend."

"Really pleased to meet you, Lady," Mr. Hodges said and immediately stood up to greet her. "We are Jesse's aunt and uncle. I am William and my wife, Edith."

Lady shook their hands politely. "I am pleased to meet you folks, as well. Jesse showed me pictures of you and a photo of him on horseback at your place. He spoke of those days as being happier times and good memories."

"Did he, now," Mrs. Hodges said. "William, it is good that he remembers those days as happier times."

"It is, Edith," Mr. Hodges agreed. "It surely is."

Mr. Hodges now became somber in his concerns. "It grieves me to bring this up, Mr. and Mrs. Parsons, and you, too, Lady. Concerning Chester today and Jesse's future. We are worried that he might try and cause a fuss. Not saying he will, but … we should be prepared."

"Sheriff Harris will be here today and he has some plain clothed fellas in attendance, as well," Harlin assured. "We had an experience with Mr. James earlier, so we are aware."

"Jesse, for one reason or another, does not want to go to the interment," stated Mrs. Parsons.

"We know that," said Mrs. Hodges. "We don't blame him one bit."

"We all went to the viewing last night and made it as quick as possible," said Mrs. Parsons. "He knows in his heart that she is no longer with us. He did not want any confrontation with his dad in the event he was there."

Mr. Hodges said, "We know, we saw you folks but waited until this morning to introduce ourselves properly and privately."

"Thank you, folks, for that," Harlin said. "Very kind of you to do the meeting this way."

The back door opened. Entered the hustle and bustle of the two youthful lads. "Hank, Jesse, please come into the parlor. There are some folks I want you to meet," Mrs. Parsons called out.

Upon seeing the boys, the Hodgeses stood up and Mr. Hodges declared, with his hand out, "My how you have grown, Jesse!"

"Uncle William, Aunt Edith?" Jesse asked cautiously.

"Yes, we are," Edith replied. Jesse went over and they had a group hug.

William backed away, "Just look at you! You're not a boy anymore; you are a man."

Edith added, "If I had passed you on the street, Jesse, I would not have known you. It has been far too long. Let's sit for a moment ... can we do that with the Parsons family? Then we must go and attend to things. Jesse, we understand that you won't be at the burial, and we are good with that and understand. But we will be back this afternoon or before."

The morning passed quickly. Gertrude and Alma were true to their word, bringing two other sisters along to help with the preparation.

Gertrude told Mrs. Parsons, "Oh my dear, what a spread you have laid out. This is so wonderful. You have gone above and beyond. And there's Lady helping out, too!"

Lady whispered to Momma, "What ... did the old crab think that I wouldn't?"

"Down girl, keep your claws tucked, just smile," Momma advised.

"Oh yes, Gertie, it is my pleasure to do service where it is needed most," Lady remarked.

"Lovely child, Mrs. Parsons," Gertrude said with a courteous smile.

People began to arrive. Pastor Richards was there to give the blessing. Sheriff Harris showed up incognito along with two plain-clothed agents, to keep the peace.

Hank and Jesse were serving; Lady was busy refreshing dinnerware and drinks. Mrs. Parsons was smiling because everything was right in the world. You would have not known it was a wake except for the large photo and other things that celebrated the life of one Ida Hodges James. People would pass by the various articles and photos of Ida. Pleasant comments were made, memories were brought to mind, and tears were shed.

Pastor Richards stood and tapped a glass. "Friends and relatives, thank you all for being here to celebrate the life of Ida. She is peacefully at rest now. It was a hard-fought battle for her, as you know. There is one standing here who helped her fight that battle—stood by her side. Her son Jesse. Let us celebrate his life as well, as he will carry on her legacy. Jesse ...."

Stammering just a little, Jesse spoke. "Yes, Momma is at peace now. I just want to say that I know she is resting in Jesus' arms right now. I, too, am at peace knowing that. And I know for sure, in a twinkling of an eye we will be together, gloriously reunited in heaven. All the pain, all the scorn that this world has brought to bear upon our family will be forgotten, and we will be made new again."

Pastor Richards asked, "Can we get an amen to that? What a brave young man ... Jesse. And now Lady Parsons has something to add. Lady ...."

"Hello, everyone," Lady began. "I am Lady Parsons. Some of you might remember me from the baptism service at the church, when I sang Jesse's favorite hymn, 'In the Garden.' Jesse fixed up this old guitar I am holding and gave it to me as a gift. I have been hammering away at learning to play the thing. He told me that he had faith that I would put some of my poetry to music. And I came up with some lyrics to fit some of the chords I have learned. The lyrics, I think, are fitting to this day—this time of remembering who Ida was and to where we stand in memory of her.

"In my Christian walk I believe that this world is not our home. In the lyrics, Biblically speaking, where the river is mentioned, it means the river of this life—the world. We still must go on within it, while those who are no longer with us have found rest, and have found peace. We as Christians bravely, faithfully go on, believing that one day we will see those we cared about in this life, in the paradise that Jesus has prepared for us. The title of the song is, 'I Will See You.'"

Strumming the guitar, Lady played some introductory chords and started singing:

Someday, someday I will see you ... walking in that paradise, where we planned to be, so long ago. But my road leads so far from home.

Today the sun reminded me that I am not alone—because somewhere it's shining from the moon through your window. And in my head I can see your face, in memory I feel that you're near me. I know that if I can reach the sun, I can wipe away your tears.

But if the fire of the sun begins to try and turn me away, I'll use the memory of your love to guide me. But my road leads far from home.

So tell me ... let me feel all your secrets ... I'll put them in a box of flowers, I will keep them near me. I will give you my heart with a picture, so you won't forget me ... no, don't forget me. We'll embrace each other, one last time to say hello, or maybe goodbye.

The river's calling me, the wind is telling me the time has come again. My love for you is real, the pain it doesn't heal, but we know it's not the end ... but my road leads far from home.

Tell me ... tell me all your secrets ... I'll put them in a box of flowers ... I will keep them near me.

The river's calling me, the wind is telling me the time has come again. My love for you is real, the pain it doesn't heal ... we know it's not the end. But my road leads far from home ... but my road leads far from home.

The song ended and there was not a dry eye to be found. "I hope the song I wrote for this occasion has captured the mood of reverence that our dearly departed friend Ida James deserves. I humbly say thank you for allowing me this moment of your time," Lady finished, and then got up to leave.

She was met on her way by William, Ida's brother. "I just want to say how thoughtful it was of you to sing for us, to put into words the emotions and feelings of this day. It is a blessing, my dear, that you have been so gifted. The Lord has blessed you. I pray you use your talent for good. Pay it forward to those in need. Touch the hearts of those who are in this tainted world, give them hope in song. I heard it, and you can do that."

"Oh my, Mr. Hodges," Lady replied, "praise be to God from Whom all blessings flow. For I can't do anything, I am nothing unless He is in it, unless God wills it to be. Thank you for such kind words."

As Lady turned to leave, there stood Jesse, holding his memories box. "Will you go with me to the tree?" he quietly asked.

"Now?" Lady questioned.

"Yes, please," Jesse beckoned.

"Sure." Lady looked around. Everybody was preoccupied. "Let's go."

Quickly they headed for the old oak tree. No time for saddling horses. They passed by the barn and down the well-traveled path they went. Lady could hardly keep up. She had never seen Jesse so determined. "Slow down, Jesse! I am not wearing running shoes," she stated. "These are new boots—and we have to cross that little stream!"

"I don't care," Jesse urged, "we are on a mission—an important one at that."

"What mission is it, that only you know about? That's not a mission at all—this is capture and tyranny!" Lady complained, turning an ankle.

Continuing without a word, Jesse sloshed his way across the almost-dry stream bed. Lady stood before the stream with her hands on her hips. Throwing off her new boots she said, "Okay, here goes!" She crossed the stream, grumbling, socks and boots in hand.

Arriving at the tree, Jesse sat firmly down, and Lady stood over him, "What is so important that we left the gathering without so much as a by your leave?"

"The box, Lady ... and you and me ... our future, or not that we have one," Jesse stammered. "I don't know if you have noticed. My aunt and uncle are here, and I am going with them. Lady ... I don't want to go," Jesse stated. "I don't want to leave you, Lady! I am in love, and if I could ... but I know I can't, I would ask you to marry me, right here, right now. If it were four years from now, I could handle all responsibilities—I could fly you to the moon and back. Lasso that—that man in the moon and bring him here—just for you. But right now, I can't."

"I will, Jesse," Lady said calmly.

"Will what?" Jesse asked.

"Make a promise," Lady declared. "I will marry you as soon as we are able."

> **"** I will make a promise . . . I will marry you as soon as we are able. **"**

"Let's bury this good memory box, then, and make a pact," Jesse suggested.

"Okay," Lady agreed. "What's the deal?"

"Our memories are frozen in time within this box," Jesse explained. "It is a time capsule to be revisited, added to, when we come back here together."

"How romantic this is," Lady commented. "Sooo cool—like something out of a romance novel. But we don't have a shovel."

"Dug the hole yesterday, in secret," Jesse stated. "Nobody knows—you and me. Twenty-five steps toward the barn from the old oak tree. Just off the trail."

They stepped it off. "I feel like a pirate," Lady said.

"You are, because you stole my heart; now it's in this box," Jesse replied.

Jesse covered up the box and Lady held him tight and gave him a kiss. "You and me, pard," she said. "We will be back here before we know it. Revisit this beautiful place of memories, but as husband and wife."

Suddenly, from the direction of the ranch, came shouting. People were running, and there was gunfire. "Oh no!" Jesse cried out, as his face went ghostly white. "It is my drunken, no-good old man."

"You don't know that," Lady pleaded. "Maybe a snake crawled under one of the canopies?"

"Yeah, a two-legged, five-foot-nine copper-headed drunk snake," Jesse stated. "I forgave him before, but not for this! No—not—for this!" Jesse took off on the run.

"NO! Jesse, let the police handle this. That's why they're here ... oooh! Stop, Jesse, please don't go there!" Lady screamed. "Oooh, these rocks!" Boot socks on her feet, boots in hand—she took off in a dead heat.

Water splashed as they crossed the stream. Jesse spied his father's truck and his heart sank. An ambulance was already coming up the lane. "Oh, this can't be good," he breathed.

Catching up to Jesse, Lady grabbed his shirt. "You can't out distance me, Jesse James. Slow down and let's look at this intelligently. It's ... not ... your ... battle."

Jesse stopped. "You are right, and whatever happened is over."

"Whew," Lady said, out of breath. "Thought I was going to have to tackle you and take you down."

The two stood and watched. There were more police, uniformed, and they had a man in cuffs. It was as Jesse suspected. There was also a man being wheeled out in a stretcher. "Oh no," whispered Jesse, "it's Uncle William." Aunt Edith was by his side.

Mr. Parsons saw Jesse and Lady and gave them a look and mouthed a warning—*go away*—and put up his hand—*caution—stay back*. Lady pulled Jesse back to the barn. "We'll go up to the loft, sit on a hay bale, and watch from there."

Once in the mow, they watched what was left of the drama unfold. Lady felt something at the back of her head and then a familiar voice. "Bang!"

"Hank!" Lady exclaimed. "Where'd you sneak up from?"

"Hey, Pard," said Jesse, "what in the world is going on? I saw my old man being cuffed ... Uncle William on a stretcher."

"Saw you two head for the barn. Smart move, guys," Hank responded. "Don't even want to get into this. Good thing you weren't here, Jesse. This could have escalated into who knows what."

"So, did my old man shoot Uncle William?" asked Jesse. "And why?"

"Apparently an ongoing family feud," Hank explained. "It involved your mom, and money that your dad felt he was owed from years ago. The fact that you are moving to Oklahoma to live was a factor. He claimed he was being railroaded, cut out of the will over something he signed off on years ago called a 'no contest' clause. It just started off as a discussion and went off the rails from there. Your dad threw food into Mrs. Hodges' face. Punched Mr. Hodges in the nose. Sheriff Harlin grabbed your dad and the whole place went nuts. No one saw it coming, but your dad had a tiny boot pistol. He pulled it and started firing; first in the air, then at the sheriff. Your uncle bravely tried to grab the gun, and your dad fired another couple of rounds, and one got your uncle in the shoulder. After that, the plain-clothes cops quickly had your dad down and under control."

"And where were you during these goings on?" Lady asked.

"I grabbed two warming-tray covers as shields and crouched behind the serving tables," Hank relayed. "I wasn't gonna take a round for nobody."

Jesse laughed and said, "Wish we had all this on camera. What a mess my old man caused."

Hank added, "And good thing, pard, as I said ... you weren't there. I was hoping you two had gone off somewhere like up here."

The ambulance pulled away. A state cruiser housing Chester James made its way out the lane. People sat around, bewildered. There stood Mr. Parsons, shaking his head. He looked up towards the hay mow's open door. He made an okay sign and motioned the young people to come down.

The three youths strolled up to Mr. Parsons. "It is a good thing that you guys, especially you, Jesse, were not around for the pinnacle of today's adventurous gathering. I can't believe it. In all my years of service in the military, in harm's way, I have never come point-blank with possible injury as I did today."

"I am sorry, Mr. Parsons," Jesse apologized. "I feel it is partially my fault that this situation came to your house."

"Not a chance, Jesse," Mr. Parsons replied, almost scolding. "Don't take it that way, son. It was Chester James. He alone brought this to bear upon this house. This is not a house of cards, and we ain't folding. We take care of our own, and that now includes you, Jesse."

"Thank you, sir." Jesse appreciated the kind words.

Both Hank and Lady gave Jesse an assurance that they stood alongside him, as well.

Mrs. Parsons was waiting under the canopy, where the fight broke out. They entered and saw the broken mess. "I guess the family that stands together gets to clean up the mess together," Hank remarked.

"Let's get to it," Mr. Parsons urged. "By the way, Jesse, I am sure you know your uncle got shot. He will be in the hospital. So you will have to stay with us until he is well enough to go home."

"Cool," Lady said. "You can go with us to the concert in Dallas. I will be singing again with Slo' Hand Scottie and The Trainwreck Survivors. Got some new material. It is the state fair, too—almost big time."

"Okay, Miss BigTime," Momma scolded. "Before y'all run off to fantasy land, I wanna see elbows. Get to it—pick up and clean up the mess. Have to get this stuff back to the rental place and I hope nothing is unrepairable. Don't know what to do about the holes in the canopy."

"Ma'am," Lady said and winked at Jesse.

BACK TO THE FUTURE AND THEN SOME

Producer Harriman checked his watch and looked at Lady, Will, and Joey the engineer.

"You are checking the time and I know we're on the clock," Lady admitted.

Seeding the conversation with his own observation, Harriman stated, "So far I have heard nothing but a nice story about growing up rather comfortable on a horse ranch. You had a neighbor named Jesse who you liked a whole bunch. His father was a drunk, abused his wife and son. Yada yada, sounds pretty American normal to me, young lady. You were the fortunate one with good parents to steer you righteous along the treacherous road of life. So what's your problem?"

"We haven't got to that yet, Harriman," Lady replied, a little flustered. "Yes, I have faults and like I said, I need to confess my transgression in order to bring a conclusion to this song."

"Oooh, Lady Parsons feeling guilty … you," Harriman chided.

"Yes, me, Harriman," said Lady. "You can be such a jerk. If Jesse and I were together today, who knows what could have happened?"

> " Yes, I have faults and like I said, I need to confess my transgression in order to bring a conclusion to this song. "

"Yeah, I know," Harriman replied. "You wouldn't be standing here telling the tale, you would be barefoot and …."

Manager Will cut off Harriman's slur. "Let her speak, Harriman, without your disdainful rhetoric."

"Just sayin's all," Harriman said. "Some intuitive observation. Even your dog understands where I'm coming from. Don't ya, boy?"

The dog sitting near Will gave a yelp.

"He's a she, Harriman," Lady quipped. "Yes, great intuitive observation you have there."

Waving at the dog, Harriman apologized, "Ooops, sorry girl."

"Can we let her continue now, Harriman?" Will asked, shaking his head.

Giving a smile and a nod, Harriman waved Lady on and she proceeded with the story.

"So the song came from small beginnings. It was one night after Jesse and I had a Bible study. It was about King Saul and David and their warlike beginnings and of course, the tragic end. Funny how I remembered that. Jesse used to always comment about the funny things that can pop up in your memory and at the oddest times.

"I can still see us talking in my old apartment back in Texas. I was leaning by the sink, Jesse was seated at the small kitchen table, and yes, there was Jesse's golden retriever, Blue, listening intently as I was spelling out my plans for the trip to LA."

SUCCESS AT A COST

Concerned but happy for Lady's meteoric rise to success, Jesse nervously stroked the head of his dog, Blue. The open Bibles on the kitchen table in front of him seemed, at the moment, set aside and unimportant this particular evening.

Forcing a smile, Jesse asked, "Is this our final Bible study, or do we just kick things around and talk about our future or lack thereof?"

Lady seated herself in front of Jesse and spoke out about how she was feeling. "I have to ask myself what it is that drives me, pushes me forward, and pushes me back. What it is about me that I can't find contentment within, right here, like other people. Momma once said to me that all I needed was right there on the farm. That out in the world people would only take and take from me until I would have nothing left to give. This is the house that built me, Jesse—the ranch, things that were taught to me ... and then along came Jesse. Our relationship, our deep friendship ... I am so afraid, Jesse."

Reaching out for her hands, Jesse said, "Until now, I have never seen this need, this concern about what might come next for you. You have always been so self-assured. You must trust me, huh?"

Smiling, Lady admitted, "Yes, Jesse, I trust you with my heart."

"You have wings darlin', and you, Lady Bird, need to fly and sing your song, leave the nest, try your wings to see if you can soar up into the sky," Jesse said. "I know that if you don't, you will have regret and I don't want to be a part of that. Even though it is a risk for me, for us, I have to go along and trust that our love is stronger than what I believe to be the grand illusion."

> **"**
> *You need to fly and sing your song, leave the nest, try your wings to see if you can soar up into the sky. I know that if you don't, you will have regret and I don't want to be a part of that.*
> **"**

Observing a new side of Jesse, Lady asked, "Now who is this philosophical poet? This is what I truly love about Jesse James—our strength and most of all, your willingness to seek understanding. Wow, you give wings to my heart."

"When you fly off to LA and the big show, do you know what I'm going to miss most?" Jesse asked.

"My red velvet chocolate cake with the butter cream frosting?" Lady offered.

"Negative," Jesse answered. "It would be our Bible studies and bingeing on popcorn ... but most of all, listening to your sweet voice trying out a new song on my tone-deaf ears. You always humbly ask me, what do you think? I like your all-inclusive kindness."

"You are so sweet to say all those nice things," Lady said with a smile. "If I didn't know any better, I'd suspect you might like me just a little."

"Always did, always will," Jesse assured her. "One of these days when you descend from the bright lights, I might be talked into making an honest woman out of you."

Lady's cheeks felt warm, the palms of her hands felt damp. She looked innocently down at the floor, away from Jesse's eyes; she paused and smiled, a girlish idea came to mind. How much she wanted to complete Jesse's dreams. She desired to revisit—to add to the good-memories box. Instead, she owned the heartache. She knew Jesse deserved better.

She picked up the guitar and said, "Since you consider yourself so tone deaf, this is a good opportunity for you to hear a new song I'm working on. You are the one who got me started by fixing up this fine vintage instrument. So you can't blame anyone but yourself."

"You are so keen at avoiding the moment," Jesse observed. "What's it called?"

"Looking a little sheepish, Lady replied, "Jesse, my dear, I think that I will simply call it 'Jesse.' The melody goes like this." Playing some chords, Lady sang the melody to the intro, "Do, da, do, do, do, da, do, do, do, da, do. I know that sounds a little corny without the lyrics but that's the intro."

"No, it doesn't. Actually, sounds pretty with you singing the melody like that," Jesse said. "Do you have any lyrics yet?"

"I have some chorus lyrics and they go like this," Lady replied and sang, "'And you know, if you need a friend ... and you know, if you need a hand ... and you know, if you're feeling down again ... come take my hand.' It repeats and I am working on the verses, but it's not finished yet."

"Suffice to say it's gonna be a hit," Jesse predicted with a smile.

Putting down the guitar, Lady smiled at his naive understanding. She stood and placed her hands in her pockets and looked down at the floor.

Then she raised her head, with a somber look. "Regret is that I never gave our song the chance that it deserved. For some inexplicable reason, other songs, but not the song of my dearest and bestest friend. So what am I saying now? You are more than a friend. I never said this out loud before, feeling that it was too fragile. Felt that if I spoke it out loud, the words would disappear. But right now, if I don't tell you, the truth will never be heard. I truly am deeply in love—I am in love with all my heart. I know that I have toyed with the words spoken between us before … almost facetiously, playing with the idea of being in love—that was so wrong. But it is different now; I have a mature understanding of the commitment. There, now I've said it. What are you gonna do about it?"

"It's not about me, Lady," Jesse responded. "It's about us. It's about giving us the chance we deserve. I've chased after you since ponytails and freckles."

"I've loved you for the persistence," Lady confirmed. "But after your mother passed away and you moved to your uncle's ranch, things changed."

"I know letters aren't the same as being there," Jesse seemed to fumble his words. Then he added, "But I kept all of yours. And when you leave here tomorrow, my pen and paper will follow."

"Did you really … kept all my letters," Lady said with a gentle laugh. "I thought I was the only one who did that."

Moving over to where Jesse was seated, Lady came up from behind and put her arms around him. "I hope we do get that chance, Jesse. I want it to be soon. I don't want time to pass without feeling the strength of your love and the trust I have in you every day for the rest of my life. I am so selfish right now. I don't make promises I can't keep. I never want to give you pain in any way. I would hurt you right now, and I could not bear that."

"There is one promise we can make right now," Jesse suggested.

"How so—a promise that we haven't already considered?" Lady asked.

"In some way, shape, or form, if something happened," Jesse spoke seriously, "and I mean if something beyond our control happened …."

Quickly pulling away, Lady took a seat in front of Jesse, looked him in the eye, and pleaded, "What do you mean if something happens—what could, Jesse?"

"Hold on, Lady, let me explain," Jesse replied. "I mean, if something untimely happened to you or me. Say, if one of us passes before the other, let the other know that what we believe in, what we have discussed, shared, and committed to—that eternity with our blessed Lord and Savior—is truth."

"What are you telling me now?" Lady questioned. "Suddenly you're not a believer anymore?"

"No, that's not it. Of course I am, Lady," Jesse asserted. "With all my heart. The good Lord knows that's in the right place."

"You know what happened to King Saul," Lady cautioned. "But as non-believing craaazy as you sound ... and because it is you who's asking, we'll seal this deal and make a pact just like the memory box."

Pretending to spit into her hand, they shook on it, sealed it with a kiss and gave each other a long hug. As they were bonded in the hug, Lady whispered into Jesse's ear, "Hey pard, wanna take me to the airport in the morning?"

"You already knew the answer to that before you asked," Jesse mumbled.

"I know," Lady responded sheepishly. "Should I get Hank to?"

Releasing from Lady's hug, Jesse grabbed her shoulders and looked directly into her blue eyes. "You are sometimes devilishly, deliciously aggravating, you know that? Of course I don't want to, but you knew that I would anyway. I will see you off, send you off, however you need to look at it."

"Stay with me tonight, then," Lady pouted. "It's too far, going back to Oklahoma. You'd no sooner get there and you would need to turn around and come back."

Producer Harriman weighed in with a loud, mimicked yawn. "Facetious, as you suggested as your concept of love; come on. I hope that's not the tiebreaker in winning my soul?" Looking at his watch again, Harriman tapped the face for all to see.

"There's much more," Lady said defensively. "But why do you have to be like that?"

"I miss back home, especially Jesse. I feel unsure about what I am doing right now," Lady lamented. "I don't feel in tune—like a dissident chord, out of touch!"

Music director Will jumped into the conversation, trying to assure Lady. "Listen to what you have created. It's beautiful."

"Am I missing something here?" Harriman questioned. "Thought these are happy praise songs, what's with the sadness? Let's move on!"

"My standing here in the flesh is testimony enough that I made it to good old Jollywood," Lady replied. "Got caught up in the glitz and glam of it all and got lost, as you know—no thanks to the fake promises of the Harrimans of the world."

> " Got caught up in the glitz and glam of it all and got lost. "

"Just doing our part," Harriman said glibly. "So what's going on with your dear old Jesse now that you faded from his sight? And if he was so enamored by a young fair maiden, how could he ever not have dogged the trail and been here with the goose laying her golden eggs?"

"Not everyone's on the take for gettin's sake," Will challenged Harriman.

"Show me one who is not willing to take something for nothing." Harriman countered. "As you well know, I have placed my 'normal' life on hold to take on this huge risk," Lady pointed out.

Harriman replied, "This history of yours is still mundane and not a tie breaker to making me a true believer."

Lady quipped, "Why are you always such a provocateur of doubt—and and mistrust?"

Harriman's cell phone rang, cutting off the conversation. "Gotta take this … but someone has to take care of business … hold on."

"Well, la-dee-da," Lady spoke out. "Here I am in Jollywood, caught up in it, lost in paradise—no thanks to people like …." She pointed a finger at Harriman. "Maybe I should have a drink, but I don't drink; maybe I should start. It's changing me—my music, too—changing the way I think and look. Oh, there's been a lot of compromising on the road—and they said my lyrics were too strong of a message—right, Will?"

"That's right, Lady," Will concluded. "Change the inspired message to make it more politically correct, to hook a broader audience. Which were the lines not worth changing?"

In answer to Will's question, Lady sang the line, "'Christ is the answer; in His promise we must believe—we are saved by grace, show your faith and through prayer He intercedes.' Make it more commercial, they said. Don't want to offend or turn anybody off, they said!"

Taking a millisecond off from texting, Harriman smugly added, "Just using our marketing knowledge, doing our part, helping out dear Lady. Don't want you to miss out on a total MOR market."

Then breaking away from his phone, Harriman leaned forward and asked the question again, "Go ahead, people—show me someone who

> "Go ahead, people—show me someone who is not willing to get or take something or make compromises simply to get ahead or get over, for the sake of career advancement."

is not willing to get or take something or make compromises simply to get ahead or get over, for the sake of career advancement. Go ahead—tell me, who? Certainly, everybody in this room is guilty in some way, shape, or form. Even you, Lady …."

With looks-that-could-kill eyes, Lady followed with a confession. "Okey dokey, mister smarty pants non-believer. I don't know why I even bother with you. Yes, Jesse has already called, trying to follow me out here, with the best of intent. But look at me now. After all the games I have played out here, I think I have already hit rock bottom. But hey, can't bounce back until ya hit the bottom, RIGHT?"

"Far be it for me to say," quipped Harriman.

"That's it for today—I'm outta here," Lady announced. "I think I will go and find a drink somewhere. Thank you, Harriman, for another fine day of standing before you, basking in your light, my eminence." She bowed and walked away.

The next morning, the phone rang in Lady's apartment. She took off her nighttime blindfold and there was sunlight breaking through the bedroom shades. She heard Maria in the kitchen. Her head was pounding as she answered the call, "What?"

"Hey, it's Harriman. Plane leaves for Phoenix at two o'clock and I just want to say …."

He never got to say—Lady hung up.

Lady grabbed the drinking glass beside her bed, took another swig of the tepid toddy and grimaced, but she drank it down and fell back to sleep. The phone rang again, "Maria, answer that, I am not here!" She looked at the clock and realized that Maria was out on her daily routine. She picked up the phone and shouted, "Harriman—I'll be there, you jerk—leave me alone!"

"Well, good morning to you, too … it's Jesse, not Harriman."

"Oh … it is my knight … goody-goody Jesse come to call … bad, bad Lady who had way too much to dream last night and took a fall. How the heck are ya there, big boy …wooo and 'scuse me for asking' in such earthly terms … but here I am. Still alive or not so much … this fine morning," Lady ended her slurred conversation.

"I am not going to state the obvious," Jesse tip-toed cautiously into the conversation. "This is not you, Lady. Say it ain't so. You are just puttin' me on, right—the actress?"

"Says me ... say so, what you hear is what you got," Lady replied. "Let me just have another."

Reaching for the glass, she missed, and it fell onto the tile floor and broke. "Ooooppsy-dooopsy, now I've gone and done it ... fine glassware and a waste of good scotch," Lady grumbled, and still hanging on to the phone, she fell out of the bed.

Fffrrr you mmpphh!

Jesse heard all of this and, now desperate, called out into the receiver, "Lady ... Lady, are you okay? Lady!"

"Oopsy ... now I've gone and fell out of the bed. Yes, my dear, I have successfully and safely landed the plane. Sobered me up a little, I'd say. Nice ceiling in my apartment ... haven't looked at it from this angle, that is to say—too much. Ha, Ha! Just kidding. Who is this again ... oh, dear Jesse. What are you doing up so early?" Lady asked.

"It is one o'clock in Texas. How is it by you?" Jesse responded, not considering the conversation disturbing reason to hang up.

"I guess it is okay, I am okay now ... better now that I am up, or down, that is," Lady laughed. "Did not want you to ever hear this side of me. But you caught me in the middle of a fight with some people, obviously thought you were someone else," Lady tried to explain. "I took some sleeping pills last night along with a hot toddy. It is a stiff drink. Thought it would help me sleep the whole night through. Guess I was right ... and then some ... whew ... didn't expect such a pounder."

"I am aware of what all that is," Jesse assured her. "I am not completely alien to the world. How about I come out to see you—maybe help out with things for a while?"

"I'd love that—but no, ah not yet, too soon for that," Lady stated, pushing Jesse off. "Too soon for you to play Sir Galahad. Besides, I will be going out of town today on a small tour with the Slo' Hand Scottie Band."

"Okay then, when?" Jesse thought he heard someone in the background; it sounded like a child. "Who's that?" he asked.

"I will let you know when. Oh, my maid Maria's back with her son. She brings him along while she works. He's not school age yet. Saves her on babysitting," Lady said.

"Cool, maybe get you used to the idea. What's his name?" Jesse politely asked.

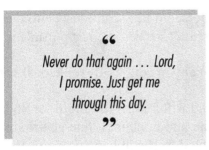

> Never do that again ... Lord, I promise. Just get me through this day.

"Got to go now ... to get ready ... see ya soon, Jesse, bye." And then she was gone.

LAX was always a busy place. Lady wore her sunglasses, hoping to shade most of the sun. Her head was still hurting, and she lamented to herself, "Never do that again ... Lord, I promise. Just get me through this day."

"Never do what again, my dear?" Harriman asked, coming up behind her.

She turned around. "Besides being a verbal jerkster, now you're sneaking up on me, too?"

"Hey, calm down. Will and Joey are with me too," Harriman pleaded.

"Oh, hi, Will; hi, Joey," Lady greeted. "I am glad you two came along. Need my pianist and a good sound man. Thank you, and I guess someone has to keep close watch on the promoters—they always try to cream off the top. So yeah, I suppose we need a guard dog, too."

"Least I'm good for something ... woof! woof!" went Harriman, and they laughed.

Lady put her hand to her head, "I have got a migraine, I think."

"I've got some pills for that," Harriman offered.

"No more pills," Lady replied. "Took some sleeping pills last night with a hot toddy and oh boy, the aftermath is a killer."

"So that's why you cranked out on me this morning," Harriman surmised. "And where'd you go last night?"

"N. O. Y. B.," was Lady's response. "Give me my ticket, please. And I hope I am seated beside Will or Joey."

Once on the plane, Lady reached into her bag for her night shade. Will told her, "So, you need to take better care of yourself, Lady. I noticed your voice was a little scratchy the other day at the studio, and a few times you went pitchy. That's not like you ... you were straining for some notes, as well."

Hesitating, Lady looked at Will. "I hadn't noticed and I ... I never do that. Scratchy ... maybe I should sing some blues, Janis Joplin style—she was from Texas."

"Yeah, but she had a sad end. I hope you don't walk down that road. Don't worry too much about it. Just an observation. Maybe the monitor setting threw you off," Will suggested and changed the subject. "It's great that you have such a good working relationship with this fellow Slo' Hand Scottie and The Trainwreck Survivors. Catchy name they got there."

"Wait 'til you get a load of their stage names," Lady chuckled. "What a hoot! But I have to close my eyes, Will."

"Sure, Lady, get some rest," Will advised. He smiled and whispered to himself, "The Train Wreck Survivors, huh ... what a hoot, indeed."

"Geoff 'The Jet' Craven plays various keys; and Sour Hickle plays the fiddle, banjo, mandolin, pedal steel, and just about everything else," Lady whispered. "If that gives you any idea."

Will just chuckled to himself.

The trip from Los Angeles to Phoenix was a short one. Will gently shook Lady as they began to circle. "Wake up, sleeping Beauty, we are about to land."

"Oh my," Lady groaned, "that was quick." She twisted around and sat up.

A stewardess came over, held out a pen and paper, and politely asked, "You are Lady Parsons—the singer—would you sign an autograph for me and the rest of the crew here on the flight?"

"Sure," Lady obliged, "what's your name, dear?"

"Amanda," the girl replied, "and flight 607—that's the short hopper you are on. We don't get many celebs on the short flights. This is so special. Thank you so much."

"You are welcome," said Lady. Then she turned to Will. "Did you bring the music to the new song, 'The Gift,' we were working on?"

"Sure did," Will answered. "Got it secured in my brief."

"Cool," Lady smiled, adding, "I want to go over it. I want you to play piano on it. Sour Hickle plays guitar, banjo, mandolin, and dobro as well; he can double on one of those."

"Talented fellow, this Sour Hickle," Will observed. "Mandolin would be most appropriate, I think."

"That's what I was thinking," Lady said.

"Great minds—great minds," Will said. He smiled and patted her hand.

"Think alike," Lady whispered. "It is so good that the Lord put us together. We relate musically and spiritually. You are an anchor in this tempest of a world."

"Just glad to set sail with you on your musical journey," said Will.

Lady whispered, "Me, too. Thank you, Will; you are appreciated."

The Survivors and Scottie were already going over some tunes when Lady and her entourage arrived at the fair. Lady unpacked her acoustic and slung the strap over her shoulder. Suddenly the rehearsal stopped.

Scottie came over and said, "Get a load of this. It is a '48 original Gibson LG-1. Vintage work. Darlin', where'd you come up with this? And why have you been hiding it?"

"It was a gift," Lady answered. "I had no idea what make or model this was. Really didn't think to ask. I use it to write songs. I love it—it is small and easy to play. I wasn't sure enough of myself until now, to bring it out."

Sour Hickle came over to admire. "They sold a lot of these back in the day. Originally came out of the Gibson Kalamazoo, Michigan, plant. If you're gonna play that tonight, we can mic it."

"Oh, I don't know," Lady said nervously. "I was gonna show you guys a new song and Will was going to play it on the piano. Sour Hickle, could you play the mandolin on it, and Will play the piano?"

"Of course, Lady," Scottie said. "We'll do anything you want. You're becoming the force that keeps our band moving from town to town. It's a fact that you are getting side-by-side billing with us and we are proud to be a part of it."

Lady laughed. "And I am proud to be on 'The Train.'"

They all got a laugh and Scottie asked, "So what's the new song? You have been coming up with some good ones."

Will jumped in. "It's called, 'The Gift.'"

Sour Hickle grabbed his mandolin and the boys and Scottie listened as Lady sang and Will played the song on the piano. They all got a copy of the music, and within a half hour they were ready for that night's performance.

"What do you think, Lady?" Scottie asked. "Where do you want to place it? It's not a jump-up-and-down song—it borders on ballad, uplifting, almost spiritual."

"Somewhere close to the end of the show," Lady suggested. "That's where Will can come out and sit down and Sour Hickle can change instruments—sort of a break in the action. Tone it down, just to build to the end."

Harriman was ecstatic. Shows were going well, offers were coming in for more. The next stop was Denver. He could not wait to hear Lady's new song performed live, to see the audience reaction. To be radio star material, or not to be—that be the question, he pondered. We need a hit, he decided.

It was time. Scottie announced Lady and she stepped up to the microphone. The crowd applauded. They came to see her, and they would not be let down.

"Thank you, folks—it is good to be in Phoenix tonight, good to see so many smiling faces!"

"Good to see you, Lady!" a voice from the audience called out.

"You folks are the first to hear my new song," Lady stated. "Y'all ready for this?"

The crowd signaled that they were.

Will and Hickle started the intro and Lady strummed her guitar and the band joined in as she began to sing.

A little boy goes runnin' by.
He trips and scrapes his knee, and he begins to cry.
His father lifts him up and whispers in his ear.
What a comfort to have his father oh, so near.

And I know when I'm alone …
You are there in my heart,
That's the gift you've given me.
We run so hard, so fast, like horses on the range.
Far away are we from the narrow gate.
Look around in fear, only see the open plain.
I feel your hand upon my shoulder, you're never far away.

And I know when I'm alone,
You are there in my heart …
That's the gift you've given me.

A little boy goes running by,
His father picks him up and raises him on high.
Running so fast, so hard against the raging tide,
Wandering as we do, we're never far out of sight.

And I know when I'm alone,
You are there in my heart.
That's the gift you've given me,
That's the gift you've given me,
The gift you've given me.

It began as a sprinkle, and then the crowd rose to its feet to bring on a thunderous acceptance for Lady and company's new endeavor. Lady waved to the band to come forward, and they all took a bow. Scottie yelled, "Lady Parsons, folks! The new kid on the block!"

Backstage, as the band came down after the show, Brad, Scottie's manager, and Harriman were beaming. "Guys, we have some great news," Harriman started to say—but stopped. "Ah, Brad, you tell 'em, because you heard it and you organized it all with the promoters."

"We have extended the tour dates because of sold-out shows," Brad boasted. "This double billing with Scottie and Lady is really taking off. The people are eating it up. Even Nashville has asked, 'When ya comin' to our city?' So, oh yeah—we are going there too!"

Scottie said, "After all these years of not being recognized—like an on-the-road vaudeville show—well, guys, and correct me if I'm wrong, but this Lady right here—she's the gift that's been given to me and us, right?"

"Thank you, fellas, for all those kind words," Lady said humbly. "But I am only as good as I am because of you guys. You are the seasoned—or the seasoning—in this musical stew. I'm looking for a good analogy here—help me out—I'm only good because you provide the experience. And Scottie, you old hobo, have been on the road longer and have paid your dues and deserve whatever I can do to help you to get ahead—all of you. We are all of us on this ride together; even if we look like wrecks, we are survivors."

The group, the managers, the roadies all gave Lady applause. "We are with you, babe!"

Scottie leaned over to Lady and asked, "You wanna sell that vintage acoustic? That's where your songs are coming from. I think it holds magic."

"Never, it was a gift—would be a sin to do so," Lady stated firmly with a smile.

"Understood," Scottie agreed, and never asked again.

Denver, Seattle, San Francisco, Omaha, Tulsa, Oklahoma City, Kansas City, and finally, Nashville. It seemed like they were on the road for a year, Lady thought, as they flew nonstop back to Los Angeles from Memphis. "It was a nice tour of Graceland," Lady said to Will. "Nice memorial to the king of rock 'n' roll.'"

"I suppose," Will said thoughtfully, "a memorial it is." Then he asked, "How are you and that fella—Jesse is his name—still gettin' on?"

"Still hanging in there. I called Jesse the other day, just to say hi and let him know I was doing fine," Lady answered.

"Hmmm. Are ya doin' fine?" Will continued, "I saw you partying with those other band guys. Need to be careful. I know what happens on the road stays on the road. There are many temptations. We have a lot of downtime to get caught up in things that we should pay no never mind to. But because we are hangin' fast and loose, we think it doesn't matter, that all we got is time. It catches up to ya, though ... those long nights on the road, watchin' the sun come up ... sleeping till after midday. Getting up and doin' it over and over and over again can make one weary. And before ya know it, you're beyond your years and all played out. Like me, a sixty-year-old black man living fame and fortune vicariously through an up-and-coming beauty named Lady Parsons. Wouldn't have it any other way, though." Then he leaned his chair back, folded his arms, smiled, and dozed off.

"Sounds like a song's in there somewhere, Will," Lady observed. "I'm okay. Thanks for being my angel." Then put on her nightshades. "Wake me over Denver."

CAN WE EVER GO HOME AGAIN?

A limo pulled up in front of Lady's exclusive apartment building. Juan, the doorman, prepared to greet and escort whoever it was in the limo. Something was going on behind the tinted windows. He was concerned because he knew, from experience, that things like that could get ugly. Finally, the backdoor burst open and it was Lady who appeared. Her blouse was open and her clothing was in disarray.

"Get back here," a male voice demanded. "You have to give to get! And you owe me already!"

Lady struggled to break free, shouting back, "What you got I don't need! Leave me alone! Let go of me!"

The gruff-voiced man seemed to be winning. Juan went over to the limo door and raised his voice, "Sir, I think you should do what the woman asked, and let her go!"

The caustic voice barked again, "None of your beez, Peeed-roo—stay out of this—this slut owes me big and it's pay up time."

After throwing the racial slur at Juan, the man let his guard down just long enough to give Lady an edge. She punched him square in the nose. He yelped and let go and Lady ejected herself from the limo, not a second too soon. The rejected man shouted obscenities, the limo door slammed shut, and the car sped off down the street. Lady stumbled on the curb, scraped her knees, and landed face first onto the sidewalk.

Juan hurried to Lady's side, "What have they done to you, my dear? This is terrible!"

"Help me, please, Juan!" Lady cried. "I don't know if I can stand. Is there anybody around? I don't want anyone to see me like this. Please! Please! Let's hurry!"

Juan motioned to Stephen, the concierge, to assist. "These chupacabras. Lady, this has to stop! You can't keep doing this to yourself!"

"I know, I know, Juan," Lady lamented.

The two men helped gather up Lady and whisked her into the office. Juan rushed to get a moist washcloth, towels, and a waste can. Juan instructed Stephen, "Go get Maria from service. She is also a nurse. Tell her Ms. Lady is bruised and bleeding. Tell Nita to take the front. Hurry!"

Lady was doubled up and sobbing. "I am so sorry, Juan ... I think I'm gonna be sick!"

"Lo siento, missy," Juan said sympathetically. "This is tragic for someone so beautiful and kind as you."

Rushing into the room, Maria shouted, "Let's get her to the couch. We should call for an ambulance!"

"No, no, no—please, no ambulance," Lady begged for discretion. "Too many questions and the paparazzi ... I can't afford that. Please just patch me up, Maria. I have fallen off horses and gotten worse than this," Lady laughed softly.

Maria chuckled, "Sí, mamacita, I will patch you up, as you say. Let me see your face. Oh, you might get black and blues. With the scrapes on your knees, you should wear black tights over my bandages. But it's not too bad, missy. I can see where a fall from a horse might be worse."

Lady replied with gratitude, "Thank you all for taking care of me."

Juan sat down beside Lady and touched her hand in consolation. "You must know that we believe you are not as some of the residents here. They walk around with their noses so high that they are at a loss to breath. When you feel up to it, we will take the service elevator and discretely help you to your apartment."

"Thank you, Juan," said Lady.

Speaking up, Juan made an observation. "If this is none of my business, tell me. I have noticed you since you first came to LA; you are different now, señorita. You have lost your inner smile. As someone who has lost their first love. You are still kind and courteous, but it has become a ritual. You are now relying on something or someone else to get you through life, and it is not the Good Word."

Lady began to sob but managed to speak. "No, Juan, it—it is you who are kind, caring enough to point out with concern what I have become. I am drowning in it. I put on a mask so those superficial people cannot see the real me."

"You gave me Bible tracts when you first came here," Juan pointed out. "Do you remember? I have kept every one of them and your business card, as well. Do you remember what it says? I keep it in my pocket. It reads—and I have memorized it—Proverbs 16:3: 'Commit thy works unto the LORD, and thy thoughts shall be established.'

"Lady, my dear, you have lost your first love, Jesus. But He is here and has not forgotten about you. You might ask, 'Well, where is He?' Lady, He is right here, carrying you through the rough times. I know you have some great responsibilities. We are here to help."

Gripping Juan's hand, Lady said, "Amen, thank you for your care."

"Now your true amigos will get you to your earthly home," Juan smiled and called out, "Stephen, Maria, vamos ayudar a nuestra hermana!"

It was a week or so after Lady's run-in with the disgruntled promoter that a pick-up truck pulled in under the veranda of Lady's upscale apartment building. It was Jesse and his faithful golden retriever, Blue. It was not typical for a slightly dented and well-used pickup truck to be parked near that fine establishment. Certainly not what the building's homeowners association would consider apropos. Blue was lying on the seat, looking up and listening intently to what Jesse was explaining.

Stephen and Juan looked on with curiosity at the Texas-plated vehicle. Juan also noted that the driver spoke to his dog. Stephen noted this as well and just shook his head.

Before going into the lobby, Jesse prepared by verbally unfolding the plan: "She is really gonna be surprised, Blue. Lady has no clue we are down here. And this looks like a really uppity-crusty place, too. Hope they let me in. She told me in a letter that she is really going through some rough times. But ya know what? See this ring, see these flowers, I'm gonna ask her to marry me. First the flowers, and then when we get to a romantic place up the coast, I'll pop the million-dollar question. Me plus you, Blue—we can't lose."

Blue's ears perked up and he seemed eager to see what might happen next with Jesse's plan. One of the doormen from the building seemed eager to know Jesse's intent, as well. Jesse got out of the truck and walked to the door. The doorman asked, "You leaving your late-model unattended, with a dog in the front seat ... for how long, did you say?"

"I'm here to pick someone up for a trip up the coast," Jesse replied confidently. "We'll be just a few minutes, sir."

"Hmmm, I hope so—good luck." The doorman smiled politely and opened the door for Jesse, adding, "You may use the house phone to call down your passenger. Do you have their number?"

"Yes sir, I have it right here," Jesse answered.

Smiling again, the doorman pointed to the phone. "It's over there. And if they say to come up, that's not allowed. They must personally come down to retrieve you or send one of their help. You are not a member here. This is an exclusive building, sir."

"Yes, sir," Jesse said and gave the doorman a polite salute. "Thanks for spelling out the rules. I wouldn't want to make a mistake, being my first time in LA."

"Obviously, we wouldn't want that on my shift," the doorman added smugly.

Picking up the receiver, Jesse dialed, all the while looking at the rude doorman.

On the other end, Lady finally answered, "Oh, what time is it?"

"Hey, Lady, daylight's burning in the hills, how is it by you?" Jesse asked enthusiastically.

Hearing the call was answered, the doorman turned on his heel, rolled his eyes, and shrugged his shoulders.

"Ya know there's a time difference, Jesse," Lady said, sounding a little put-off by the wakeup.

"Not from where I'm standing," Jesse told her.

"Really, are you here in town?" Lady asked.

"I'd be knocking on your door by now, but security is tight," Jesse explained.

"You are in the lobby—stay right there—I mean give me a few and I'll be right down." Lady's tone had changed; she sounded almost glad that he was there. "We'll do something, go somewhere, breakfast, brunch, lunch, whatever time it is, don't matter."

"Wherever the day takes us, sweetheart ...." Then there was a click and Jesse didn't get to finish his sentence; he just looked at the dead receiver he held in his hand. He looked over at the doorman and said, "I guess she's just in a hurry to see me."

The door man remarked, "Obviously, sir. But then again, good things come to those who wait. Lucky you."

"You are so right, sir," Jesse said, when suddenly the elevator opened and Lady appeared, wearing a scarf and sunglasses. She approached and saw the bouquet of flowers Jesse was holding.

"How beautiful and thoughtful of you. Thank you, Jesse!" Lady seemed suddenly perky. She looked at the doorman and said, "John, please call us a cab so Jesse and I can go down to the pier for brunch."

"Right you are, Lady, and quick as a jiffy," John the doorman said, ready to comply with the request.

Hesitating for a second, Jesse spoke up, "Hold up John, let's not and say we did. We have my transportation." Jesse turned to Lady and asked, "Do you know the way to San Jose?"

Smiling at the conversation, John stepped aside and opened the door for the couple and Lady saw Blue in Jesse's old pick-up. She burst out, "You are a poet, Jesse James, and … you drove all the way out here in your pick-up with Blue. Let me give her a hug, but you first."

Doorman John smiled and finally gave Jesse a job-well-done nod and a wink of approval.

Embracing Lady, Jesse said, "Yes, the old truck made it here and so did Blue. She kept me awake most of the way, but gave up somewhere around the Rocky Mountains."

As Jesse, Lady, and Blue left the smog in the rearview, Lady gave Blue a hug and said, "This is so cool, Jesse, so unexpected. I have always wanted to do this. How did you know?"

"Didn't—but it is so good to see your perfect smile again," Jesse said, being a little proud of the fact he caused it to happen. "Seeing you here beside me, that alone is worth the price of admission."

"You believe that you have to throw down to spend time with me?" Lady smirked.

"Not what I meant, and you know it." Jesse clarified, "I knew if I would call and ask if I could come out to LA to see you, you'd come up with all kinds of excuses—too expensive, save your money, too tired, have a show … just too this and too that, just too busy … Well, here I am, and you have no excuse now."

"Can't think of one right now," Lady mused and grabbed hold of Jesse's hand. "I am overcome with … I am exactly where I want to be right now … being whisked away by my knight in shining armor."

Smiling, Jesse remembered the time Lady went with him to the fair and they had their photo taken. It was one of those magic moments locked in time. "I am right where I want to be at this very second, Lady, sharing this day with you."

Lightly touching Jesse's cheek, Lady nodded approvingly and spoke softly. "Yes, we are, Jesse, right where we should be. I don't want this day to end. We can just keep driving and driving until the wheels of this old truck fall off. And whenever that happens, we can just keep going, you and me and Blue and never look back; leave everything that's bad and ugly behind." Lady's voice suddenly changed; it was shaky as she pleaded, "I so want to be happy, Jesse. You lift me up, you make me happy. I feel secure with you." She held on tightly to Jesse's arm.

Curious, Jesse thought to himself, *Where is all this coming from?* He glanced at Lady as he asked, "What's up with the scarf and sunglasses? Are you afraid to be seen, or that you might be recognized? You haven't turned into a vampire, have you?"

"I'm not a vampire," Lady assured him. "Too many late nights in the studio and back-to-back shows have taken a toll on my looks. I wanted to ease you in on my aging problem."

"Come on, cut it out," Jesse said persuasively. "This is me, Lady. Seriously, I want to see your face."

Lady removed her scarf and let it fly out the window. Then she took off her sunglasses, revealing a bruised eye. Jesse quickly pulled the truck to the side of the road as Lady looked down at the floor of the truck, knowing that the drama was soon to start. The first teardrop of the day cut a trail through her make-up, dropped to her skirt, and she asked quietly, "Don't judge me too harshly, Jesse, please."

"What is that?" Jesse questioned. "I want to know. Tell me the truth, because this cannot stand. I believed that these were good Christian people you were coming out here to work with. I knew there were hard times ... but this?"

"Oh, they claim to be; they are, but some, he claims to be, but at times …. Oh Jesse, you are kind, and with you, what you see is what you get. But here, it's not always clear. I get wrapped up and confused and I give my trust too soon. I am like the little moth to the flame." Lady grappled with the next sentence and punched the dashboard with her fist. "Oooh, I do want to go home ... but I can't."

Jesse paused for a moment then said, "Trust is something that must be earned—if you can't trust someone in little things …"

"How can you trust them with the greater?" Lady finished. "Sounds easy to do when you say it."

"Point the abuser out to me," Jesse said. "I guarantee he will never, ever touch you again, and that's my promise."

"Maybe it is, I have brought this upon myself," Lady said sadly. "Maybe I deserve this. Maybe, Jesse, you never knew me at all. Maybe it is, you should take me back ... drop me off where you found me today. Could be there's a big reason I did not invite you up this morning?"

There was a pause in the conversation. Traffic whizzed past the parked truck, and then the horn of a semi blasted a warning and broke the silence.

"I see," said Jesse. "Is that what you want—to be left out here all alone, forgotten by everyone who cares about you? There's nothing redeemable about this LA town and there's nothing here for you but sorrow."

A few more tears found their way down Lady's cheeks, making a floral pattern on her skirt. Without looking at him, Lady pressed her hand to his and said, "I saw the signs for Ventura. Let's go there and find a place to eat and talk for a while. Would that be okay with you?"

"Sure," Jesse agreed. He started to say something more, but stopped, put on the turn signal and eased the truck back onto the highway. All were silent on the drive; Blue stared out the window, Lady looked straight ahead, her arm tightly wound around Jesse's arm. Jesse kept his eyes on the road and his hands on the steering wheel. Deep thoughts swirled inside his head. He pondered whether the admission price was worth all this.

Once the two were seated at an outside table with an ocean view, the tension seemed to ease a little. The sun was shining, and you could watch the gulls flying about, fishing for their next meal. Looking around, Jesse smiled and said, "This is a really nice place, Lady. Wow, you've got everything you dreamed of coming your way. Truthfully, what more could you possibly need or desire? From my understanding, you could retire right now and go wherever and live wherever you want. I hear Hawaii is really beautiful year 'round and it's an easy plane ride from the coast."

Looking through her sunglasses at Jesse, Lady caught a hint of disdain in his last statement. She addressed the issue. "Sure, you think I can write a check and sign off on everyone and everything, and done. How cold do you think I've become? Oddly, right now, I am flat broke. My luxury apartment, so safe and secure, complete with the pompous doorman. Poof! Could be gone next week if I don't throw it down. Like a hooker, john to john, I live concert to concert. Once you rise to a certain level, you have the obligation to maintain it, to keep up the show, the facade."

"I know you are hurting on a level that I don't or can't comprehend from where I am sitting," Jesse replied, trying not to sound demeaning. "Our enemy, Lady—yours and mine—is the prince of lies. He wants us to question who we are. He asked Eve, 'Did God say you should not eat from any tree in the garden?' His suggestion was that she was found wanting, in need, missing a piece to a puzzle. Then, ever so sly, the creature cleverly stated, God knows that when you eat it, your eyes will be opened and you will be just like Him'—Genesis 3:5. Remember our long nights in study? So please, Lady, confide in me, what could you possibly be missing in your life, that you are so lacking, so desperately in need of? Perhaps it might be the return of your true identity. Because the girl I see sitting here ... you are not the same person I put on the plane a while ago. Who are you?"

Nervously, Lady fidgeted with the napkin and dropped the silverware onto the floor. "Jesse, it would be kind of you, if you would take me back to my apartment."

> "The trick is to live in this world and not to be part of the system of things," Jesse pleaded. "While we are subject to its rules, we need not be subjected to it."

"The trick is to live in this world and not to be part of the system of things," Jesse pleaded. "While we are subject to its rules, we need not be subjected to it."

Sipping her water, Lady's jaw tightened at Jesse's last words. "No kidding, Jesse! As I said … it all sounds so easy coming from you. But you are not the one standing up to their hips in the mire. Oh, just take me back, why don't you?"

A waiter came to the table and replaced Lady's silverware. He pointed at her, smiled in recognition, and was about to say something when she stopped him short, "No, I am not who you think I am—just someone who resembles her."

"Riiight, okay, yeah I'm cool with that," the waiter responded. "Would you like to order something, whoever you are?"

"I will have the cali-veggie salad, the tomato bisque, and a glass of your best sherry, please," Lady ordered.

"And for you, sir, what may I get for you?" the waiter asked with a smile.

"I will have the California burger platter with the works and anything you might have cold on tap with a frosted mug," Jesse said.

"Coming up in a jiffy," the waiter said.

Looking over the top of her sunglasses directly at Jesse, Lady pleaded, "No, Jesse."

Speaking to the waiter, Jesse threw up his hands and said, "Hey, when in Babylon, do as they do, is how I see it—right? I wouldn't want to be called out for being abnormal or anything. I want to fit in … go along to get along, don't ya know?"

Perplexed, the waiter said as he backed away, "Alrighty then, I'll just leave you two to your conversation and I will place your orders now, if you don't mind?"

Making a shooing motion, Lady turned back to Jesse. "Is this some insane attempt at being spiteful to gain attention? You've already pricked the kink in my armor. You had my love and my heart a long time ago, and you have my ear."

"Nope, no rancor on my part," Jesse assured her. "Just prepping for the long, winding road that leads home, because I realize there's no room at the inn for me here—going to where I belong, Lady."

Lady sat quietly, searching Jesse's eyes. Then she reached across the table and touched his hands. Around them ocean waves rolled in, seagulls called out, utensils and glasses clinked together, diners conversed, and time momentarily froze. The food arrived and broke the connection. Looking down, Lady at first ignored the salad and Jesse grabbed a few fries and jump-started the dialogue. "I believe in us, Lady. You and I are a team. We had a calling to bring some light into this dark world, to bring comfort to those who were abused and in need of sanctuary. We had plans, didn't we?"

> *You and I are a team. We had a calling to bring some light into this dark world, to bring comfort to those who were abused and in need of sanctuary. We had plans, didn't we?*

"Yes, we did have some wonderful dreams, Jesse," Lady agreed. She pushed a folded piece of paper to him and added, "This is a poem, perhaps to be a song in the future. It might be considered a lamentation."

"Was it just my dream?" Jesse asked. "I thought we shared that belief to make it happen. Perhaps it was just me alone, and I should have asked you first before going ahead with those plans?"

"What plans are you talking about?" Lady asked.

"Oh, nothing right now," Jesse said, unfolding the message. He read it in silence.

My Mask
Lady Jane Parsons

Cold-hearted sphere that rules my life, my privilege takes a twist so sad.
Fettered soul, no comfort from innocence stolen, I alone must take it back.
Put on the mask I thought myself, the act will always show me smiling.
Place my face behind a veil, the curse that falsifies my blue true feeling.

Lies paid off in dividends, within my world arrived so many friends.
Just me and Precious Mask, 'Oh, joy,' that I would now be one of them.
Fool not myself into belief that folly behind the mask would hide.

> Accompaniment by sweet charade so dear, holds something
> amiss deep inside.
>
> Shuttered stillness, pale of night, no one close to hear the cries.
> Sitting on my nightstand watching, is by day guardian of the lies.
>
> Welcome sleep washes over me as numbness
> Drowns the pain from which there is no healing.
>
> Alas, oh curious friend, designed they well
> The joker sitting upon the throne, who justifies the letting.

Holding back the tears, Jesse commented, "I am so sorry for your pain, Lady. Maybe I have been too judgmental. Through this 'lamentation' as you call it, I find your reasoning."

"Hey." Lady reached out to touch Jesse. "We had the light; we really did, and it shined between us. But sometimes that light does not rest upon us and win over the darker venues of our nature, but that is why God gave us grace, isn't it? We stand and we fall, we pick ourselves back up to stand again, but only through the grace of God, here go we. Did you not always tell me that?"

"You are so right," Jesse confirmed as he reached into his pocket, pulling out a small red velvet box. "This is for you, Lady. I've never had anyone to trust in this regard. You have always been honest with me, as you are now; even if the medicine was tough, I always knew where I stood."

Taking a forkful of salad, Lady stared at the tiny box. She remained silent but curious and then whispered, "What is that?"

"It is something for you to think on, maybe consider. When you are ready … I will be waiting, as I have been, time after time," Jesse said.

"I love that song, Jesse. You know, that has been your song—yes, you have been waiting for me, haven't you—time after time," Lady said, smiling.

"Oh, come on, the guy's a sap," said Harriman, almost laughing. "Good thing you did not buy into that program. He would have ruined your career. Obviously, you turned his boat toward open water and told him to shove off."

"You are one cold cut." Lady threw up her hands and scolded, "How in the world do you sleep at night?"

"Very well, actually," Harriman answered. "And thank you for asking. I don't take to heart the bleating of every lost sheep I come into contact with. I can't save everyone. There's how we perceive life should be, and there's everything else … I call it reality. Welcome to California."

"Oh, I see how it is. He ditched you," Harriman said with a chuckle. "After he saw all the baggage, it was bye bye."

"Wrong again, Harriman," Lady countered. "I let him down when I said this life I lead, even though it will probably finish me early, I can't stop it. And the happy dream we once shared was gone. Oddly, all I live for now is the approving smiles and applause of strangers. I sing and play to those that appreciate me enough to listen. Street corner or concert stage, it doesn't matter."

> The happy dream we once shared was gone. Oddly, all I live for now is the approving smiles and applause of strangers. I sing and play to those that appreciate me enough to listen.

"Talk about cold, Lady, you ran your friend aground on an emotional iceberg," Harriman observed. "That's one icy bon voyage speech. I would surmise that he left your life for good at that point."

"Outta sight but not outta mind," Will told Harriman. "Lady's heart went with Jesse. I think he had a mishmash of feelings when he headed east. He was all wrapped up like a ball, wound so tight he wouldn't unravel until he reached home. Right, Lady?"

Shaking her head, Lady tried to explain. "As one very caring human being, Jesse was woven so taut with frustration because I wasn't taking his calls. I suppose that my rejection at that point drove him back to his father's way of handling things—he started drinking."

ALMOST HOME

Sitting in front of Sheriff Harris's desk was something new to Jesse. He explained the fix he was in from his point of view. "Look, Sheriff, I really haven't been myself lately. Ever since getting back from the trip, I've been beating myself up a lot. I just need some time to get back into my work."

"You took one hard fall off the wagon you were riding, staying sober for so long," Sheriff Harris commented. "And that's great. Don't let the matter of … well you know, eat away at ya; you're better than that. You built that beautiful new house up there on the hill on the property your momma left ya—did ya tell her that? She doesn't even know, does she? You and that big pride of yours—it's as broad as your shoulders. But you ain't Atlas."

"I almost told her about the house I had built for us, but I hesitated. And I'm sorry, Sheriff. Something I don't remember, though, and wonder—did I hurt anybody?" Jesse asked. "I'm not mad at anyone in particular, just mad at the world, I suppose."

"Nah, and if you did, they've already forgiven you," Sheriff Harris said. "You know, that's how it is around here—everybody's knowin' your business. That's why we're just talkin' and you ain't sittin in the uncomfy seat behind bars. Have ya even tried calling Lady … just to talk … nothing wordy or uncomfortable—just chit-chatty stuff?"

"Hardly know where to begin right now," Jesse answered. "I've tried, yeah—but she's not answering."

"She will, son, she will." Sheriff Harris said. "When she does answer, ask her how it's going. Tell her you are doing fine; even if you're not, tell her that. Don't let the last words you speak to each other be in anger or remorse. Tell her you still care and that you are here for her but that you understand that she needs to be where she's at and that you need to move on with your life."

"Sheriff, that's a lie," Jesse disagreed, almost in anger. "Look at me, I'm all torn up ... pieces of me are still back there; I ain't doin' so fine. I haven't left LA and what I saw there in the rearview. You have no idea—she was literally beat up and refused to admit it. Is her pride doing this? She said that was where she wanted—no, needed—to be. Who in their right mind wants to live in hell? Tell me, Sheriff, she's not right in the head ... she don't even remember her right mind."

"Right now, that's not your call to make, son," the sheriff advised. "She has to deal with it on her own terms. She's like an addict, but in a different way. Lady's like an addict waiting on the bottom of her own situation before she can bounce back and admit, 'I have had enough.'"

"Time, love, understanding, and prayer are what Lady needs right now to work it out on her own. She'll either come back or press on. Everything we do comes with a price."

> **"**
> Time, love, understanding, and prayer are what Lady needs right now to work it out on her own. She'll either come back or press on.
> **"**

"Tomorrow, after I have rested from this ordeal and gathered up some courage, and I don't mean from the bottle," Jesse stated, "I will absolutely and resolutely take your advice, sir."

"Good," Sheriff Harris replied. "Lady's got the spine of a strong-minded woman. We all know and love her from back here in the hills. If you would have tried forcing Lady to come back home before she was ready, she would have hated you for it and bucked like a horse being broken. There would have been no peaceful living with that woman that way, and you have to know that. Now get outta my sight and don't come back here by way of arrival as you did last night."

"Don't worry, Sheriff, I'm headed for the mountain, bypassing the watering holes along the way," Jesse declared. "I got a date with Blue, the comfort of the fireplace, and some much-needed downtime."

"By the way, the weather forecasters are saying there are some severe ice storms headed our way tonight," the sheriff advised, "so as you said, go and hole up for a few days while this thing blows through."

Standing up, Jesse offered his hand. "Thanks, Sheriff, for being understanding. I'm taking the first steps at coming back to my old self."

"You always were the comeback kid," Sheriff Harris noted, chuckling. "You'll land on your feet and be as good as new. Be safe up there in that shanty on the mountain."

Leaving the Sheriff's station behind, Jesse returned to his truck, where Blue was anxiously waiting. Jesse unlocked the door and gave the dog a hug. "Blue, you are the best. What do you say we head for the house and get some chow for me and you and kick back by the fireplace?"

Blue gave an affirmative bark as Jesse slipped behind the wheel of the pick-up and fired up the engine. As they left the blacktop behind and started up the gravel mountain road, the rain he had been cautioned about started to fall and then freeze on the windshield. Jesse turned up the heater in an attempt to defrost the window. Turning on the radio, Jesse heard a song he liked, and sang along with it. "'It's the gift you've given me.' I know I can't sing very well, but I like the song 'cause it reminds me of Lady and our times back on her poppa's ranch. Those were some great times, Blue."

Squinting in order to see the road, Jesse kept talking to Blue. "Man, the Sheriff said we'd be in for it. It's hard to see the road; good thing we are almost home."

Blue gave another approving bark and Jesse continued, "It's funny how you remember things, Blue, and at the oddest times. I remember those good things—they're never far out of sight of the memory's eye. Just like you, Blue, you're always by my side, never far out of sight, are ya?"

Lady and her production team held a meeting. When asked about how things were going in her life, she explained some recent events. Harriman wanted to know why the song, "The Promise," which they were giving a final nod on to consider it finished, was such a major concern.

About her personal life, Lady was brief. "Oh, Jesse has tried to reach me time and again," Lady confessed. "But hey, let's get down to the business at hand. All these years between Jesse and me brought about the song originally, but that's not how it stands today."

After being prompted to tell them the original lyrics, Lady got a faraway look. She seemed to need to be in the past in order to portray the emotion needed to relate the song in its perspective. She started out partly speaking the words to lead into song. "A friend had called me, said, 'This eastern weather's killing me ....'"

Lady's voice wavered a little and she paused. Getting up from his chair, Will went over and laid his hands on her and said, "You don't have to go through this, you know."

"Let me be, Will," Lady replied. "They need the entertainer. So let me entertain."

Sitting back down, Will looked at Lady. His eyes welled with tears as she started again. "A friend, they called me, said, 'This eastern weather is killing me.' You know, I told that friend to come on west and see about me. If you need protection from the wind and rain and cold or if you're feeling down because that scene is getting old ... don't you know, if you need a friend ... yes don't ya know, if you need a hand ... and you know, if you're feeling down again ... come take my hand—I'll be your friend."

"So the original version of the song, you had it shelved," Harriman speculated. "Because you were inspired to do a rewrite. The lyrics, the melody lines you just sang, are so like the new version in many respects. People love melancholy songs. Why fix it if it's not broke, was my way of thinking. But it is okay that you turned it into a praise song. That works well, very good, by my standards. I just hope the promoters and buyers can sell it."

After the day's meeting, and putting the song 'The Promise' to bed, back at her apartment Lady started to think about finally making the commitment and putting her personal life together. I am so ready now, Lady thought. Tomorrow I am calling that big lug and I am going to invite him out here so he can sweep me off my feet and take me home. Lady whispered loudly, "YES! I WILL MARRY YOU, JESSE JAMES! I want to scream it so loud that it will bounce around and echo through those hills back home. I am almost home, Jesse ... no, we are almost home!"

In the morning, Lady took the red velvet box from her nightstand, opened it, and smiled. She took the ring from the box, placed it on her finger, and, as ladies do ... moved her hand away and turned it over to get a good look. This made her smile even more. Picking up the wedding band that she'd purchased the day before for Jesse, Lady held it up to the light to admire its workmanship. "Not too fancy, not too plain; Jesse will like this," Lady said out loud. Feeling pleased, she headed for the shower and planned the call that she felt would change her life forever.

Just as her hair was toweled dry, the phone rang. Lady saw from caller ID that it was Momma. Again Lady picked up Jesse's wedding band, held it tightly in her hand, and considered telling her mother about the decision. But she hesitated; when Momma called, it was usually very important. "Hello, Momma ... I know because you are on caller ID. What's wrong, why do you sound upset? ... Are you okay? ... Oh no, what happened to Poppa?"

Momma was breathing heavily, trying to get the words out. "You wanna think about taking the next plane home. And I mean today."

"Momma, I've got a concert tonight ... I got bills to ...." Lady was cut off in mid-sentence.

"This is not a multiple choice, girl." Momma demanded, "Cancel the concert."

It was a serious emotion that electrified the telephone line all the way to LA. "But Momma ... why, what is going on ... tell me, please," Lady pleaded as emotion, dread, and fear became almost tangible.

"Ain't no way out of sayin'," Momma replied, choking on the words. "It's Jesse, honey."

"Oh my, he works 24/7, never quits to rest .... Is he sick? How bad could he be hurt, he just needs to take it more easy, but I will call him. In fact ... I was going to call him this morning ... I'll do that as soon as we hang up, Momma ... I am going to tell him I will ...." Lady's chain-link rambling was broken.

"Hush up, girl—listen to me," Momma commanded. "Not sick, not hurt ... JESSE'S DEAD!"

Lady gripped the receiver, feeling dizzy. She whispered the last few words, not realizing she had already hung up the phone. "Next flight out, Momma ... the very next available ... I promise." Slumping like a rag doll to the floor, she sent the wedding band from her limp hand bouncing across the tiles. It rolled and rattled until it hit the wall, wavered about on its circumference, then silence.

In the meantime, Momma, not knowing, spoke to the hum of a disconnected phone. "I will send your brother Hank to pick you ... hello ... hello, Lady?"

Flying home seemed further from reality than anything Lady could have imagined. She had dreamed that the next flight home would be about wedding dresses and bridesmaids. Life turns on a dime, Momma would say, and that expression seemed very appropriate at this time. Thinking of the good times back at the ranch, she remembered how they rescued Jesse, the dinner, the poo-bag story, and how they laughed. Replaying the night at the fair and the photos they had taken brought Lady heartfelt joy as well as a mist to her eyes. Jesse confessed to Lady his concern about his father's drinking problem, and wondered if he had done enough to help him. This brought a lump to her throat. Staring out the window from 26,000 feet made her feel insignificant, and Lady wondered if that's how God sees us, so tiny, so frail, so vulnerable.

Then she remembered Jesse's strength through faith and the first time he silently prayed for all of them at their kitchen table. Lady stepped out and did as he had done: "Oh Lord, give me the strength to bear this homecoming. Lord, only you can shore me up, for I am weak and I have been so far removed from you. Please give me grace; forgive me, Lord, for my sins and trespasses. I am fearful to face all that I feel will come to bear upon me. Lord, I know you hear my petition and may it be Your will to grant me such, in Jesus' name. Amen.

At that moment, Lady heard and felt the vibration of the landing gear being brought into position. She had not even heard the pilot's announcement that they were close to landing, and her heart fluttered as the wheels touched down for a safe landing.

Upon disembarking, Lady heard a familiar voice calling out, "Lady … hey, Lady … over here!"

Running with bags in tow, Lady gave her brother a huge hug. "You are a wonderful sight for these tired eyes. I have missed you, Hank. Still unmarried, still working with Poppa … and such a good-looking guy as you … how have you managed to stay unhitched?"

Laughing, but ignoring the question, Hank said, "Been a while now since you left the ranch, and on the drive here, I was thinking about all the mischief you and I used to get into."

"Me, too, said Lady. "But that was always you getting into trouble and me taking the fall or bailing you out, Hank. Let's get the story straight."

"Yup, suppose I was," Hank confessed. "What say we get headed on down the road. You are staying at el rancho, casa de Las Parsons, of course?"

"Sí, hermano," Lady said with a smile. "Tengo hambre. Can we stop for a bite to eat?"

Chuckling at Lady's Spanglish, Hank replied, "Sounds bien—I'm hungrier than a starving boll weevil trapped in a rotten cotton patch. How about a drive-through? You want a burger with fries, or a taco, or what?"

Lady laughed. "You were always great with the descriptive analogy. I'm a vegetarian now, Hank—plant based. Really, I'm vegan," Lady admitted.

"You're an alien what?" Hank asked. "I hope it's not contagious. You grew up on a horse and cattle ranch, are you delirious?"

"Nope," Lady stated flatly. "My order will be a veggie wrap and a fruity smoothie, thank you very much."

"Oh, no," Hank chuckled. "Poppa will think it un-American, and hard tellin' what Momma will say." Pulling out from the taco stand, Hank lovingly threw two veggie wraps toward Lady, and comically held his nose while he handed her a "fruity smoothie."

"I sure don't know much about Cali-for-ni-a, but from what I can tell after spending the last half hour with you, Lady, it scares the beeswax outta me," Hank stated.

"Oh, come on now," Lady replied. "Just changed my diet a little bit so I can keep my voice in good condition. But I must ask—since I haven't been home in a while, has much changed?"

"You mean Poppa? Why do you think to ask that?" Hank asked.

"He never liked my music idea," Lady answered.

"I bet if you searched hard enough, into all the places you shouldn't be snoopin'," Hank suggested, "there's where you would find a scrapbook containing all your adventures."

"They always had me on the short leash," Lady mused. "Don't do this, do that. Don't go here, go there. It's too dark, it's too cold ... not until you're eighteen you don't, and then when I'm eighteen ... nope, not until you're twenty-one."

"Maybe you've got it wrong, Lady," Hank suggested. "They were concerned because they didn't want to see you get hurt. As you now can testify, it is a big, bad, ugly world out there. How's your faith holding up, because over the next couple of days it's gonna get tested."

"Oh, I've been a bad girl, Hank," Lady confessed. "On the plane I prayed—something I have not done in so long that it felt awkward. I will be tested for sure. Can you play the big bro once again and hold my hand, if needed?"

"Of course, that's what an hermano mayor is for," Hank said with a laugh. "You knew that Jesse built a big house up on the mountain, didn't you?"

"We spoke about doing that one time," Lady said, trying to remember. "So maybe vaguely, but I don't think so. I can't remember for sure."

"So he never came right out and told you?" Hank asked.

"No," Lady replied.

"That'd be just like Jesse," Hank observed. "So you know, he was building it for the two of you. He had this big idea of you coming home one day, living happily ever after, making a retreat for less-fortunate children—a safe haven as he called it."

There was silence as Lady set her vision on the road in front of them and Hank could see a tear running down her cheek as she barely whispered, "Did he tell you that's what he was doing?"

> **"**
> He was building it for the two of you. He had this big idea of you coming home one day, living happily ever after, making a retreat for less-fortunate children—a safe haven as he called it.
> **"**

For some reason, Hank looked down at Lady's left hand; her ring finger revealed a diamond engagement ring, and now it was Hank who took a deep breath as he swallowed hard to find the next words. "Aahh, yes, Lady, we did talk after you left for the big show."

"And you never told me," said Lady. "So I would not have known, how could I, as no one ever said a word. I guess you all felt allegiance to Jesse rather than your closest kin."

Hank was backpedaling now, not knowing how to move on, when Lady did it for him. "So what ever happened to Jesse's dad?"

"Cirrhosis of the liver," Hank replied. "The cancer finally got him. Ironic ending for him, wouldn't you say?"

She's oddly pensive, Hank thought, noting the change in Lady's countenance. "Yes, I would agree about Chester's demise being ironic."

"Yup, but Jesse was never into any of the shenanigans his dad was into," Hank stated. "You know—the bars, heavy drinking and womanizing, if that's what you were thinking."

"Never thought that in any way, shape, or form about my Jesse." Lady tersely added, "But they do blame me—don't they?"

> **He loved you, but you loved something more for a time.**

"Oh Lady, maybe," Hank said cautiously. "Only the ones that don't know any better. Come on, it's not your fault—so don't go there. Jesse was his own dog, and yes, he loved you, but you loved something more for a time. Still it ain't your fault. He was willing to wait 'til your attraction for the stage lights would grow dim."

Hank felt as if he was about to fall into some mental abyss. He kept looking over at Lady and back to the road ahead and back at Lady and back to the road. Something was cooking, he could see it, he could feel it.

"Need to know, Hank," Lady blurted out, startling Hank. "You've been avoiding the million-dollar question and answer. You ain't volunteered anything—what really happened to Jesse?"

Yup, there it was. What Hank was most fearful of, and he answered cautiously. "I'll try making it brief … no, Jesse was not drinking, and I'll make that positively clear from the get-go. It was a freakish, nightmarish ice storm that came through here. Kids should not have been in school in the first place, and they were let out early. It was black ice, nasty, roads like a mirror, and there it sat in the middle of the road. It was a bus caught sideways, and couldn't go forward or back up. And it was on one of those tight turns where you start up the mountain. Around that corner came

> **He was willing to wait 'til your attraction for the stage lights would grow dim.**

Jesse and Blue in his pick-up truck. To avoid hitting that bus, Jesse took his truck down over the side. Oh, he tried to jump out ...."

Seeing the tears in Hank's eyes, Lady continued, "But what ...."

"Lady, the door closed on him," Hank cried out. "Oh, I did not want to be the person to tell you this."

Tears welled up in Lady's eyes. "Who then, Hank, if not you—who would tell me?" Lady almost shouted.

Hank wiped his tears with his sleeve and Lady grabbed hold of his arm as she slid over beside him. Hank put his arm around Lady and said, "Aren't we the brave and tough ones, huh?"

"On an odd note," Hank said through sniffles, "witnesses said that poor Blue tried pulling Jesse to safety and stayed with him until the ambulance and medical team arrived. But nobody has seen hide nor hair since ... as if she knew it was over, and that nothing more for her remained."

"Oh, poor Blue, she must be somewhere. We have to look for her, Hank," Lady said. Then she perked up, "Hey look, there's the ranch coming up."

"Yup, and there are Poppa's new horses," Hank said, pointing enthusiastically, trying to bring lightness to a somber story. He added, "He believes he has some winners right there."

"He's such a gambler," Lady said.

"He might be, but it keeps him young," Hank noted. "Besides, what else would he do?"

"Good question, I know," Lady agreed. "Hey, you got a shovel in that toolbox back there?"

"What the world do you need a shovel for?" Hank asked.

"Instead of gambling, I'm going prospecting," Lady answered with a smile.

Rolling his eyes, Hank chuckled. "Same thing, but what are you digging up?"

"Something," Lady said, with an air of mystery. "Turn down the pasture lane and go to the old tree hangout."

"I guess you wouldn't know, but it got struck by lightning last summer and Poppa cut it down," Hank reported.

"Really, Hank, is nothing sacred anymore," Lady said sadly. "Just humor me, okay?"

"Of course, whatever you want," Hank complied. "Still know how to boss, don't ya?"

"Somebody's got to keep it in line," Lady replied. "Wow, Poppa has increased his stock. Horses on one side and a whole bunch of cattle on the other and this must be due to your helping out. Not retiring yet, that's for sure—look at this spread."

The rutted pasture road produced a bumpy ride. Lady looked out in admiration at what her father and brother had done with the place. "It's beautiful, Hank. So pretty out here," she remarked. Arriving at the stump of the old oak, they got out of the truck and Hank retrieved a small camp shovel from the toolbox and handed it to Lady. "You the all-knowing boss, now you dig."

Staring at the offer, Lady retorted, "Hhhhmmph, you the unknowing wouldn't know where to begin anyway. Give me that silly little thing." Looking around, Lady realized she didn't know where to dig, either. "With all this brush I'm not sure where the tree stood."

Smiling, Hank pointed and said, "Well, little sis know-it-all, stump's over there, if that helps."

"It does, yes it does," Lady said, giving Hank the waspish eyes.

Lady pushed back some brush as Hank looked on. When she finally came to the stump and stood on top of it, she proudly announced, "Avast, matey, the treasure lies just over there in that direction, some twenty-five paces." Hank folded his arms and rested against the truck as his sister marked off the steps and said, "Right here, Hank, I'm certain of it."

"Uh-huh, show me, but watch out for the rattlers, copperheads, and water moccasins," Hank advised.

Beating the brush as if to scare away any slithering creatures, Lady finally pressed her foot to the shovel. Lady smirked at the nonbeliever who asked, "Are you sure you don't want me to do the honors?"

"What!" Lady exclaimed. "You think because I'm vegetarian now that I've lost my cowgirl—is that it? I always could out-ride, out-shoot and out-rope you, tenderfoot Hanky pants."

"Who you calling tenderfoot Hanky pants, lil' sister?" Hank called back. "If you're not careful, I'll come over there and take that shovel and whoop you with it."

"And do what?" Lady asked loudly, slightly out of breath. Then there was a clanking sound. "See, Hanky pants, I found it!"

"You call me Hanky pants one more time, so help me," Hank warned, going over to where Lady had dug up her treasure chest.

"I won't, I know how much you hate that," Lady said with a smile and held up a black plastic bag that apparently contained what she was digging for.

"Is that what I think it is?" Hank asked.

"Yup, it's Jesse's good-memories box," Lady answered as she took it from the wrap and eagerly held it out.

"Unbelievable—it's been here waiting all this time," Hank said in amazement.

"Yeah, we buried it here the day of his mother's funeral, just before he went away to his uncle's ranch," Lady explained. "Been here all this time, and I almost forgot about it."

"How come I didn't know about it?" Hank asked. "I could have accidently, not knowing, plowed it up."

"It was a secret between Jesse and me," Lady said proudly. "You are my brother and although you know just about everything about me … some things a girl just has to keep close to her heart."

Once again seated in the truck, Hank started the engine and said with a smile, "I understand Lady, I really do, but are you gonna open it, or what?"

Lady had considered doing just that, but she stopped. Seeing a tear rolling down her cheek, Hank grabbed her hand. "And if you don't right now, that's cool, because as you said, some things a Lady has to keep just for herself. Let's take you home again." Hank put the truck in gear, and they bounced their way back across the pasture road.

"Just when you feel all shiny and new and believe you have it all figured out … BANG! An inconsiderate driver unwittingly hits that mud puddle of life and splashes its grime all over your new white dress," Lady lamented.

"Ain't life just like that," Hank agreed.

"And thanks for your understanding all these years," Lady said solemnly. "You always picked me up when I'd fall. You'd say get back on that horse, Lady, you can do it.… guess I'm rambling?"

"Nervous?" Hank asked. "The fear we don't face limits us. Don't be afraid because I think it's gonna be a blessed parent and child reunion … and it is surely needed. Remember our lives are short even in its longest day. So tread lightly, be patient, and savor every moment with love and care."

As the truck was nosing into the final approach, the long driveway to the house, Lady said, "Ain't it a hoot how weddings and funerals bring people together, and I wanted a wedding?"

"That's a fact," Hank agreed and then looked at Lady with curiosity.

Excitedly Lady called out, "Look, there's Momma! She saw us coming!"

"And Poppa, too," Hank added.

"Truth is, Lady, they tidied up your old room for ya."

> "
> *Ain't it a hoot how weddings and funerals bring people together, and I wanted a wedding?*
> "

Before the truck was fully stopped, Lady had the door open and she bolted from the truck. She was well on her way to falling into her momma's open arms, and her poppa embraced them both. "I know, I know, baby," Momma said.

Sobbing into her mother's shoulder, Lady apologized, "I am so, so sorry!"

Poppa asked, "For what, darling. You've done nothing wrong."

Lady slipped from their embrace and spoke plainly. "Yes, I have—I purposely shut you out! It was as if I was embarrassed. I've kept you at a distance, and I am so ashamed. Well, it stops right here, right now. I didn't know how wrong I was until we turned into this old dusty lane that has brought me back home again. I didn't know how much, I mean how much I love you and need you … in my heart I realize that this is home. I have never left you, Momma, I have never left you, Poppa. You are eternally right here in my heart." Lady broke down, fell to her knees, and began to sob.

Momma and Poppa rushed forward, picked Lady up, and Momma spoke out, "Oh, darlin', we understand now, and we always did. You never said, so we never asked. Because this is your journey, sweetheart; we thought it was what you wanted."

"It was always what we thought you wanted to do," Poppa said. "Why would we think any less, or love you any less, for chasing your dream. We gave you a good start, the rest we trust to the Lord. We prayed that the seeds of faith that we planted would find fertile soil and take root. These are heartfelt times, but with prayer and standing together, we're gonna make it through."

Proudly standing and sporting a huge smile with Lady's luggage in hand, Hank said, "See, I told ya, Lady, this was going to be a much-needed reunion and it would all turn out right. Now what shall I do with these bags? Are we gonna stand out here wading in happy tears, or go inside for Momma's sweet lemonade?" Without waiting for an answer, Hank proceeded up the steps to the house.

Looking a little dumbfounded by Hank's dialogue, Poppa said, "Why not? Let's turn these salty tears into honey-sweet lemonade." Happily reunited, arm in arm, Momma, Lady, and Poppa followed Hank's lead.

DRAMA AND GRIEF

A bright beautiful morning it was, but the occasion was solemn. The Parsons family pulled up to the white country church where Jesse's funeral was to be held. It was the same church where, years earlier, he had been baptized. Attendance was in order and most were standing outside, chatting before the proceedings began. Oh, how funerals and weddings bring people together, as Lady had said.

"You know, Gertrude," Alma began, in a high tone, "that Parsons family was never part of the good folks from around these parts. 'Horsey people,' I calls 'em. I think they're from Tennessee. No good can come from there, ya know?"

"No, I think they're from Kentucky, Alma," Gertrude corrected. "But nothing good comes from there, either, if you want my opinion. The northern influence, if you catch my line of thought."

"Saw it right off," Alma said. "That high-minded daughter trampin' off to Hollywood—sin city that it is."

"Yes, let the truth be known, Alma," Gertrude affirmed. "The way she let poor Jesse out of her life and on his own, flat on his face and high and dry, is what she did."

"She did, Gertie," Alma said with certainty. "She sure did, shook him off like a cheap suit for the bright lights ... and after he went and built that mansion just for her."

"Cost a million dollars, from what I heard," Gertrude added flatly. "Wonder where you come up with that kind of money ... hmmm?"

"Maybe she paid for it?" Alma speculated.

"Where'd she get it?" Gertrude asked with a smirk.

"Sold herself to the demon, many are sayin'," Alma proposed slyly. "Look at all those crazy people out there—they claim to have demons serving their purposes. That's what gives them their unnatural powers."

"Unnatural powers—to the devil, you say?" Gertrude asked.

Rocking back and forth on her heels, Alma smiled and whispered, "Yup, but you didn't hear all this from me."

Gertrude smiled and assured Alma, "Oh, you can count on, me Alma. I'll not breathe a word. Your information is safe with me."

The demeanor of the two changed suddenly as the Parsons family arrived. Pleasantries were exchanged as Mrs. Parsons was the first to greet. "Hello, Alma—Gertrude, it is so sad of an occasion to be meeting like this."

Smiling and nodding sadly, Alma replied, "It is a very sad time, indeed, Mrs. Parsons. How is poor Lady holding up? Oh, there she is, poor thing. So sorry, Lady, for your loss, and we must have tea before you go back. Only if you have time, of course, as I am sure you have a very busy schedule out there—hectic I'm sure, but let's chat, shall we?"

Responding with a polite smile and nod, Lady seemed to wobble as Alma finished her greeting. Momma placed her arm underneath Lady's and held her close as she whispered in her ear, "Pay no mind to those witches. If you hadn't noticed, I am sure you have. There are twice as many faces here as there are bodies—sayin' one thing and thinkin' another. Be brave, honey, and this, too, shall pass. Just give it up to the Lord; we are here to pay our respects, not start a war."

> " There are twice as many faces here as there are bodies — sayin' one thing and thinkin' another. "

Sheriff Harris grabbed Mr. Parsons' hands and held them in his as he said, "These surely are sad times and we have lost a good citizen of this county. I also want to thank you and yours for what you do for the less fortunate of this area. You attach no strings or even notes to it, but I know it's you, sir—thank you!"

"Thank you for saying, Sheriff," Mr. Parsons replied. The Sheriff hesitated as if he wanted to say more, but he moved on.

"The Sheriff looked like he had more to say," Hank said to Poppa.

"Maybe he knows something more about Jesse and all," Poppa said, almost thinking out loud.

Music played softly in the background as friends and family came in. Hands were shaken, tears were shed, hugs were generously applied, and kind words were dealt out abundantly. Soon everyone found a seat and Pastor Richards rose to start the service.

"Dear friends, neighbors, brothers and sisters," the pastor began. "We have come together to pay our last respects to our friend, our brother in Christ Jesus, Jesse. I have known Jesse for many years. Even through tragedy and much adversity he remained steadfast in his belief of our Lord and Savior. Whenever something was in need of repair here at the church, you could count on Jesse. He repaired, replaced, and painted, never asking for anything but to serve. Jesse was a true man of faith who simply and humbly was here to help.

"I shall read one of Jesse's favorite passages. It is one that he went to often in time of need. These verses, he said, gave him assurance and comfort—John 14:1–4, 6—Christ's promise to return:

> Let not your heart be troubled: ye believe in God, believe also in me. In my Father's house are many mansions: if it were not so, I would have told you. I go to prepare a place for you. And if I go and prepare a place for you, I will come again, and receive you unto myself; that where I am, there ye may be also. And whither I go ye know, and the way ye know. ... I am the way, the truth, and the life: no man cometh unto the Father, but by me.

"And if I may in conclusion recite First Corinthians 15:54–55, 57:

> So when this corruptible shall have put on incorruption, and this mortal shall have put on immortality, then shall be brought to pass the saying that is written, Death is swallowed up in victory. O death, where is thy sting? O grave, where is thy victory? But thanks be to God, which giveth us the victory through our Lord Jesus Christ. Amen.

"Our brother is now resting. Jesse is waiting for us to be reunited with him. If there are others here today who wish to share a brief thought about Jesse, you may do so at this time."

Standing up on wobbly legs, Lady began her walk, moving forward, holding Jesse's good-memories box in her hands. Her mother said a silent prayer to shore her up, and her father wiped a tear from his cheek. Hank smiled with encouragement and gave Lady a thumbs-up. Alma nudged Gertrude and said, "Well, look at this, won't you."

Upon reaching the platform, Lady turned around nervously and cleared her throat. She sat the box on a stand beside the podium, smiled, and spoke to the congregation. "My name is Lady Parsons. I want to assure everyone that I have spoken to the pastor and all close relatives, clearing with them that what I am about to say and do is appropriate."

The pastor remained behind the podium and said, "It's okay, Lady; please come over here and stand beside me."

As Lady came close to the pastor, he gave her a hug and put an arm around her as he again addressed the congregation. "Over the past several days I have come to know Lady better. My friends, she was close to Jesse and probably closer to him than anyone could imagine. She is a brave young woman. Please, everyone welcome her."

Moving back, the pastor sat down and left Lady alone to speak. "I know that many of you have mixed emotions about me. Probably many are not interested in what I have to say, as you will think it a confession rather than an expression of my admiration for this young man who has been consumed by fate so early in life. I deeply loved and cared about Jesse."

Lady picked the box up from the stand and opened it. "This box I am holding is Jesse's good-memories box, which we shared as teens. It contains memories of his childhood—photos of his family and photos of Jesse and me at the county fair. There are poems and letters he wrote to me and letters I wrote to him. As I said, this is his good-memories box."

Pausing to regain her composure, Lady sighed and took a deep breath. She looked at her mother, who was in tears, but she pressed on, her voice slightly wavering as she began again. "The final contribution to the box I will make today, and there are three; the words to a song I wrote to Jesse, which I will play in a moment." She demonstratively placed the paper in the box and added, "And two: this tiny jewelry box that contains the engagement ring that he entrusted me to wear when I was ready." Lady placed it in the box.

Stopping for a moment, Lady continued, "And finally, in my hand I hold the wedding band that I purchased for Jesse, as I was going to say yes to his proposal. But that plan was cut short when Momma called to let me know that I needed to fly home immediately because of the matter for which we are all gathered today.

"Not even my family knew about my wedding intention ... I am sorry, Momma, Poppa, and all. It was my own private and personal decision. When my brother asked me what I was going to do with the memories box the other day, I told him that there were some things a girl must keep to herself. Yes, I loved Jesse. He was kind, loving, thoughtful, sincere, and honest. There is no one I have ever met that I wanted to spend the rest of my life with, or give my undying love to. In tribute, I will now play the song I wrote for him."

There was not a dry eye in the church as the pastor approached the podium and, holding up his right hand, said, "Heavenly Father, watch over, accept, and give peace to Jesse now. We ask travel mercy to all attending. Bless us all, help us with our loss and mourning. We hold up our petitions in Your Son's precious name. Amen."

Be careful, everyone, and we will see all those who wish to attend, at the gravesite."

Moving the piano seat up, Lady began to play the song of tribute, "The Promise." People stood to leave; a few remained to listen, but as most do, they rushed to file out of the sanctuary.

A curious man in a pin-striped suit and black horn-rimmed glasses carrying a briefcase tried to push his way inside. The outpouring of people was too much and forced the man to halt. The lot attendant told him that he had to move the limo from the front of the church. This upset the man, who reluctantly returned to the limo.

Back inside the church several people came forward after Lady finished the song. Momma, Poppa, and Hank rallied around her in support. One woman shook Lady's hand and said, "Jesse would have been proud of you, honey. What you did took courage and you hardly wavered from the task."

"Cat's outta the bag now, Sis," Hank remarked.

"Oh, perhaps not all of it," Lady said quickly.

"Brave little sweetheart," Momma said, gently stroking Lady's hair.

"You let it all hang out, honey," Poppa said with raised eyebrows. "I could not have done what you did. You brought a lot of closure to the ill will brought on by those old busybodies ... but then again, who knows ... better yet, who cares, right?"

Hank and Lady both got a chuckle from Poppa, who expressed concern as they made their way out the back of the church. Lady saw the pallbearers loading the casket into the hearse. Suddenly she was overcome, as butterflies and goosebumps came over her at the same time. Noticing her stumble, Hank held her up and said, "This funeral thing is normally sad, Sis. It'll be over soon and we can call it a day, go home, and regroup." Poppa and Hank helped Lady into the front seat. Then Momma took her place and Hank started the van.

"Not as bad, sad, as you thought it would be, or was it worse?" Hank asked, trying to redirect their thoughts by jump-starting conversation.

Speaking first, Lady answered, "I'm sad, of course. But it's the fact that I know people want to say something to me and they hold back. I sensed it by their eyes walking all over me ... that's what made me sick. I wish they'd just say it, let it out, so we can have at it and call it a day."

As they pulled up to the gravesite, Lady grabbed Hank's arm and said, "Can we wait just a minute before going over there?"

Poppa laid his hand on Lady's shoulder and so did Momma as she said, "Sure, Lady, we can sit here for a while, can't we, Poppa?"

"As long as you want, right, Hank?" Poppa asked.

"Right here suits me fine," Hank replied.

From the van, the Parsons family watched as the graveside service unfolded. Saying the words with Bible in hand, the pastor performed the last rights. Family members stood in the front and close friends behind. One after the other came forward, touched the casket, and laid flowers on top.

Now Lady opened her door and moved toward the gravesite, Momma and Poppa on either side, arm in arm, and Hank in the lead. Held tightly in her hand was a single red rose. People parted as they approached, and the casket began its descent. Lady had waited until last to place her rose, and she picked up a handful of loose soil. As she leaned over, Lady dropped to her knees and could not help but cry. Momma, Poppa, and Hank surrounded her. Onlookers stared while others departed, shaking their heads with hushed comments. Speaking quietly, Lady said ever so softly between sobs, "They don't understand. They know nothing about Jesse and me. Lord, forgive them."

After Lady placed her flower and handful of soil, Hank and Poppa helped her up and they began to make their way back to the van. Hank noticed that the only ones left at this point were the grounds keepers and a curious little man standing off to one side. He watched them intently. He held a large black briefcase in his left hand.

The Parsons family was halfway to the van when a voice shouted out, "Excuse me, excuse me—are you folks the Parsons and are you the young lady … well, Lady Parsons? I recognize you from your photograph, I believe. I'm not a fan, but I do need your signature. I sense this is bad timing and all—but I need to get back to Chicago. We are facing a deadline, HEY!"

The fact that they kept walking, not paying attention, really upset the briefcase man. "PLEASE, I really need to speak with you, Ms. Parsons. It is truly important—not for me, but for you!"

Catching up to them, the man became obstinate and demanding. "HEY, LOOK—this is very, very important! I hold here Jesse James's last will and testament, and you, Lady, are his one and only heir. I will not leave until we go through this process right here and now!"

Now Lady stopped and turned around and looked at the man. "I don't want it! I don't want a thing from or out of this tragedy!"

The man replied, "It's not about you anymore, or what you want or don't want, young girl. You can do with it as you see fit. Nevertheless, you are the heir."

Out from the briefcase the man pulled out paperwork, all the while speaking. "Please sign these documents. Then you can live in it, sell it, rent it, make the house and land into a foundation on the deceased's behalf. It does not matter—it is up to you."

"What about his kin?" Poppa asked. "Won't they kick up a fuss?"

"A fuss!" the man responded. "Searched and in due diligence found no one else mentioned anywhere, and no other will exists, present or past. If you are thinking about a pending contest, they haven't legs to stand on." Handing a pen to Lady, the man asked, "Please sign in these places, here, here, and here, so I may go back to civilization."

Hurriedly Lady complied and signed the documents atop the makeshift briefcase desk the man offered.

The man's demeanor suddenly changed as he said, "Aahh, now that wasn't so bad was it? I know it is unorthodox doing this on the day of the interment, but my whole journey concerning this legal case has been just that, edgy. Now I thank you; here are the keys to your inheritance and have a wonderful life. Everything has been paid for and laid to rest, so to speak."

Turning on his heel, the briefcase man started to leave, but halted and turned back. "One last thing, though, so I am not remiss, and this is actually in the will. You must see the house and verify that you have done so within twenty-four hours. Call the number on the card and let me know, or the entire will becomes null and void. There are conditions but could not tell you until after you signed ... ha, odd request I know, and that now is the long and short of it. I thank you all ... happy life, ciao!"

With briefcase in hand, the strange man now ambled back down the hill to a waiting black limo, going back to what he deemed civilization.

Alone once again, the Parsons family, stunned by what had just taken place, watched as the limo pulled away. Poppa mused, "Odd sort of duck."

"Ain't he though, huh," Hank agreed.

"Now don't that beat all." Momma added.

Lady looked in disbelief at what was left of her earthly relationship with Jesse and said, "I guess this is it—a copy of the will, a deed and a set of keys, and of course, Jesse's good-memories box." Managing a sad smile, as if for the whole day Lady had been holding her breath, she finally exhaled and half joking asked, "Are we there yet?"

THE INHERITANCE

"That's where it happened," Hank pointed out. There had been placed at the scene of Jesse's accident a small cross with flowers. "That's nice that someone arranged a small memorial," Lady said. "'In Loving Memory' ... I wonder who did that—it should have been me."

"Don't even start this morning with the negativity," Hank warned.

"I won't be negative from here on out, I promise," Lady replied, pretending to zip her lips.

Laughing at that, Hank said, "Good, then we are on the same page." He added, "I can't help but think about what the briefcase man said ... as soon as possible ... within twenty-four hours."

"That is curious," Lady agreed. "Have you ever been up here?"

"Nope," Hank answered as they closed in on the last hundred yards of the bumpy mountain road to Jesse's house. Turning one final corner, the huge pine trees gave way to the building's site. Hank stopped the truck abruptly. Sliding to a stop almost sent Lady into the windshield. "Whoa, Hank," Lady shouted, placing both hands on the dashboard to stop herself, and then she looked up.

"Wow," Lady exclaimed. "This is something else ... it's beautiful, Hank. I might have to cancel my promise, just to shed a few tears of regret and joy."

"Yup," Hank replied, "I mean to agree with the 'wow' factor, but not on the regretful tears."

"It's a converted A-frame structure built into the side of the mountain," Lady commented, stating the obvious. "Pull up closer, Hank, and let's go inside."

They walked up the stairway, and the front of the house made Lady think of the bow of a ship. With the huge stone outcropping of the fireplace and glass, lots of glass, and the view from the huge front porch, you could see for miles. "Wow!" Lady exclaimed again. "I can't take this all in at once. I think I'm going to faint. How could you do that, Jesse James—going and dyin' on me!"

"Don't go getting wheezy on me," Hank warned. "The hospitals are way too far back that way."

"Let's open the front door instead," Lady said with a smile as she inserted the key and turned the knob and they stepped inside. "Wood," Lady observed, "everywhere Hank, and look at the workmanship in this place. Oh, Hank, oh Jesse ...."

"What's that noise, Lady?" Hank asked.

Turning around, Lady listened and quickly headed for one of the doors in the kitchen area and said with a smile, "No way, Hank! That's an animal scratching at the door. How could it be ... but I'll bet it's Blue!" A bark of affirmation was given when Lady said Blue.

When Lady opened the basement door, out popped the jailed canine showing happy affection as Lady hugged her. "How in the world did you get here, Blue?" Lady asked. And as she turned to look at Hank, they shouted at the same time, "THE BRIEFCASE MAN! TWENTY-FOUR HOURS!"

"Who would've believed it?" Hank reflected. "Blue was always by Jesse's side."

"She will always be at my side now," Lady said. "Blue is my guardian angel."

Blue gave an agreeable bark and Lady and Hank laughed. Lady got up from her kneeling position and gave Blue an invitation, "Come on, girl, take me on a tour of your home." Walking around the house, opening door after door, Lady finally ended up at the dining table. In front of the centerpiece there was an envelope addressed to her. Lady picked it up, opened it, and began silently reading the letter that was enclosed. Then she stopped. Looking around, Lady noticed Hank looking out the windows, admiring the view. "Hank, you wanna come over here and listen to what I am about to read?"

"Sure," Hank replied. "What is it?"

"A letter from Jesse ... postmortem," Lady answered as she slumped into a chair with Blue now resting comfortably at her feet.

Before beginning to read, Lady demonstratively held the letter in the air and asked, "How would he suspect, or even think about, such things as this?"

"He was proactive, not reactive," Hank responded. "To be forewarned is to be forearmed. He was looking at the possibilities—our next breath is never guaranteed."

"I get it," Lady said, showing a little stress as she began to read out loud. "'Dearest Lady, I am writing this letter several days after completing this house. If you are reading this, it is because we can't be together right now. My attorney would have placed it as instructed, and if time is being kind, Blue is there, as well.'"

Pausing for a moment, Lady looked a little angry and said, "You know, Hank, I guess now anger is part of the grieving process, and that is exactly what I feel right now. Somehow I think that all this tragedy could have been avoided. I don't know how, but that is what I feel."

"The IF factor is huge," Hank said. "But it never seems applicable within reality. It never plays into the here and now."

"I guess that is true," Lady agreed, "but this is too weird, as he wrote, 'Yup, I passed before you did and I had hoped we would have shared a whole lifetime together, but it wasn't meant to be. I love you so much, but never said those words enough. It is strange the things we remember and at odd times. Since ponytails and freckles I have adored you. I told you that evening before I put you on the plane.'"

Shaking her head, Lady said, "This is so unbelievable. Hank, it is like he knew this. It goes on to say, 'Whatever wrong passed between us and for whatever reason, if it was my fault, please forgive me. And as corny as this might sound, because I love you, you never had to say you were sorry for anything. It was never about how much you loved me, but that I loved you enough. Being in the faith gives us an advantage.'"

Grimacing at the words, Lady put down the letter and looked out at the view from where she sat. Hank said, "He sure did give a care about you, Sis."

"That big dumb guy and his corny words ... yeah, he did," agreed Lady. She continued, "'Hold on to that faith,' he goes on to say, 'the faith that we both shared and studied. As it has for me, faith will also carry you through whatever life throws at you. Remember John 14:6—I am the way, the truth and the life: no man cometh unto the Father, but by me.'"

"Via veritas vita," Hank said.

"That's right, Hank," Lady said. "I had no idea you would know that."

"Lotta things you don't know about me, Sis," Hank replied. "I read a lot—my mind hasn't been idle since you left. Finish the letter."

"You must elaborate sometime," Lady said.

"Like you said," Hank reminded her, "some things are best kept close to the vest. Now finish, before I get all choked up." Puzzled, Lady looked at Hank and continued, "Okay ... 'This house can be a blessing for you, Lady; use it as a refuge, a sanctuary, to get away from the madness. It is

> This house was built on faith and prayer. It can become a hope for many, if you use it to praise Him. Do this with your talent and music. Make everything you write, praise our Lord and Savior, Jesus Christ.

God's and my gift to you. It was built on faith and prayer. Do not take this blessing lightly. It can become a hope for many, if you use it to praise Him. Do this with your talent and music. Make everything you write praise our Lord and Savior, Jesus Christ. Did you ever do anything with the song you wrote for me? I never heard the song. Don't make it a song about me. Make it a song to praise God. Love, Jesse.'"

Engine noise could be heard approaching and a car appeared. "What and who in the world would be coming up here?" Hank asked loudly, feeling a little put off. "No one would know that anyone would be here, let alone live here."

Getting up from the comfy chair, Lady looked out the window as a late model car pulled up and a young lady got out. As she looked around, she seemed perplexed. Then she turned around and saw Hank looking down at her. She smiled and waved and walked over to the steps and started toward the front door.

Hank looked over at Lady and said, "She's coming up, whoever she is." Hank went to the front door and, turning the knob before she could apply knuckles to wood, opened it. "And how may we help you today, young lady?"

"Oh my," she said, waving her hand in front of her face with surprise and asked, "Is Lady Parsons at home?"

"Who should I say has come to call?" Hank asked.

Nervously the woman answered, "Kally, that's Sally with a K, ahh, McCoy ... Kally McCoy, from her old high school days." She ended the sentence smiling, and nodded for approval.

Turning around, Hank addressed Lady, "You know Kally McCoy from high school?"

"Yes, sorta in high school," Lady answered, "But hardly knew much about her."

"Well, she's come to call," Hank said. "Do I let her in, or don't I?"

"I guess, yes, of course let her in," Lady replied, somewhat curious.

"Well, come on, Sally with-a-K McCoy," Hank said with a smile.

Trying to find the words to explain the unannounced visit, Kally sheepishly began with an apology. "I am sorry to barge in like this, unannounced. But I have come a very long way, actually. I now live in

Asheville, North Carolina, and have, ever since we graduated. I know I haven't seen you since high school and all. But I have been called, no—driven to see you in order to deliver a message."

"Please have a seat so we can all be relaxed," Lady invited, pointing to the couch. "Hank, help Kally find a seat."

"Sure," Hank said, "Where are my manners? Over here, Kally. You must be very tired from the trip. Would you like a glass of water?"

"Yes, that would be wonderful," Kally replied. "I'm not some crazy fan, Lady, although I do like your music. So it's not an autograph I'm looking for—no, that's not the reason I'm here. Oh, I don't know how to say this so that it doesn't sound contrived, or that I'm looking for something in return, nothing like that."

"Well, it's important, I gather that," Lady said. "How did you find me, way up here?"

"Oh, that was the easy part—your mom," Kally admitted. "First I drove to the farm. I remembered that from our graduation party."

"My dad had that all arranged," Lady said, remembering. Then she smiled. "That was very cool of him to do that, of course, he had graduating twins—and me."

"Your parents were really neat people, from what I remember," Kally remarked.

"Yes, they were—I mean, they still are," Lady said. "I mean, they're not dead, so yeah—they still are."

"Getting a little confused, Lady," Hank said, laughing.

"Oh, thanks for the water," said Kally.

Hank took a seat on the opposite end of the couch and Kally continued her narrative. "I guess you are dying to know what this strange guest wants of you. I mean, it's not so much about what I want, but apparently what someone else wanted."

"How so, Kally?" Lady asked.

"First, let me tell you that I am a strict Christian, raised in a Baptist home with a southern upbringing. I don't dabble where the Good Book says not to tread, and I am a loving mother of two daughters and a devoted wife to my husband, Frank. He and I own a successful mom-and-pop paint and wallpaper business. So, all that being said …."

"We are not questioning your honesty or integrity, Kally. We can see that you are not about nonsense and you've taken this journey for good reason. Right, Lady?" Hank assured their guest.

Deep in thought, Lady looked up to say, "Yes, Kally, please go on."

"Well, it was the day or so after your friend Jesse passed away. I mean, that news traveled by my phone grapevine like wildfire," Kally continued.

"I confess that this is about a dream I had that has brought me to your front door. You know how sometimes you work so hard that even at night you dream about it?"

Chuckling, Hank realized what was implied. "Oh, I'm not laughing about what you said, but I agree with what you just asked. I dream about horses all the time … it's what I do—train 'em, feed 'em, break 'em, ya know, all the time—so yeah, I too dream about my work."

"Come on, Hank," Lady scolded.

"Just sayin's all—it's what I do," Hank said, shrugging his shoulders.

"Sorry, Kally. Please go on," Lady encouraged.

"Well, I was up on a ladder on a landing at the top of the stairs," Kally went on to explain. "It was the exact same place where I had stopped working that day—a surreal continuation of where my day had ended. I took up where I left off. The downstairs door opened, and up the stairs came three young gentlemen. Curious, I watched them come closer."

Lady listened intently and began to feel uneasy as Kally continued. "First in line was Jesse. Then my first husband, and finally, another young man who was killed in a car accident when we were still in high school—Harman something or other. Anyway, all three mechanically said hello as they passed me and entered the living room area of the apartment we are papering and painting. I continued to paint like nothing was wrong, when suddenly it hit me—they're all dead …. Well, you can imagine my surprise at that. I immediately came down from that ladder like a shot and marched directly over and stood with my hands on my hips. There they were seated—one, two, and three on a couch, and I asked them straight away—what are you doing here—you're all dead!"

Kally started waving her hands in front of her face. "Wow, this story gets me so worked up!" Kally quickly took a sip of the water.

Taking on what the soldiers call the thousand-yard stare, Lady sat looking through the big glass windows, apparently taking in what Kally was relating. Then she broke the silence with the obvious follow-up. "What was the reply?" Lady quietly asked Kally.

"What?" Kally asked.

In an almost forced whisper, Lady shuddered as goose flesh crept up her arms and she asked again, "The reply, Kally … what was the reply?"

"Jesse looked at me, smiled, and said, 'No we're not … we believe in His promise and we are only sleeping.' I did not get a chance to answer him because then I sat bolt upright in bed. The commotion woke my husband, and he asked me what was wrong. In those few seconds, it dawned on me that that message was for Lady Parsons. My husband told me that without delay, the message must be delivered. So, Lady, consider it delivered!"

Choking, gasping for air, Lady doubled over and cried out, "Oh, dear God, how much more?" She raised her hands to the sky and petitioned, "I ask ... I pray that you send me an angel, not to take away this pain but to give me the strength to endure! Yes, Lord, I believe in your promise, I do—from here on let it not be my will that is done, but in all things, Your will that leads me on! Christ is the answer, in His promise I believe; I will show my faith—I am saved by grace, through my prayers He intercedes! Amen and amen!"

Still on her knees, Lady tried to find composure. Kally and Hank stood over her and looked for some kind of sign that she was okay—otherwise, she needed help. Fanning herself with her hands, Lady said, "I'm okay, I'm okay, all this was somewhat overwhelming."

"I hope my message was not all that upsetting, Ms. Parsons," Kally said. "I believed it not to be of a dark nature, although things of this sort could be misconstrued as such."

"I don't think that Lady thought that at all, Ms. Kally," Hank assured her.

Getting up, Lady placed a hand on Hank's shoulder for support and looked at Kally. "My dear Kally, you have brought closure to something that was promised a long time ago. You have no idea what you have just done. You and your message have been a blessing."

"I am glad for that, Ms. Parsons," Kally replied, smiling. "I really am."

Sitting back down in the comfy chair, Lady looked once again at Kally and offered, "If you want, you may spend the night with us and continue back home in the morning. I'm not a hundred percent sure what is here to eat, but I am sure we can find all we need. You are welcome to stay, is what I am saying."

"That's very kind," Kally replied, "but I must get back. I have stayed long enough to deliver the message, and that's what was needed—so I must be on my way. Again, thank you both."

With that said, Kally turned and started to leave. Lady got up and followed behind Hank, and at the door, Kally turned and the three hugged. From the porch, Hank and Lady waved goodbye to their mysterious guest. Hank said just before going back into the house, "You know what, Lady ... I'd not be more surprised, if while sittin' on the privy a hand had reached up outta there and pinched me on my back side, than just hearin' that story. That blew my mind, and that is for certain."

"Now that is creepy, Hank," Lady commented; "I mean your analogy, not what Kally just told us."

They started to go inside and Hank said, "I know it, but it sure was a surprise." Changing the subject, he asked, "So what did you find in this mansion to sleep on?"

"Two bedrooms, fully furnished," Lady answered. "The master for me, of course, and the guest for you, Hank. There's food in the fridge and dog chow on the basement steps, so I think Mr. Briefcase was instructed to bring things up to status quo."

Lifting up the receiver of the wall phone and flipping the light switch, Hank gave Lady a wink. "Phone works, lights are on, and there's running water. What more do you want? Let's spend the night and see if there are any more surprises that await us. I'll call Momma and let her know what we're doing."

"Sounds good. We can do more exploring in the morning," Lady agreed. "And you make breakfast."

Clanging and banging on a pot Hank called out, "Calling all sleepyheads … wakey, wakey, eggs and fakey bakey time for all you veg heads!"

"Who are you calling sleepyheads and vegheads?" Lady said with a laugh as she and Blue came through the front door. "We were watching through the window to see if you really were going to cook breakfast. We went for an early walk so we are ready for some food. I didn't know you knew how to cook, and where did you find the veggie bacon? But I know what you're going to say … there's a lot of things …."

"You got it—now park it and let's eat," Hank instructed. "Oddly, there was a pack of this stuff, 'vegan bacon,' in the fridge. It really tastes fakey."

"Okay enough about the fakey bakey. Where's the real jelly for my toast?" Lady asked. "Can't have toast without jam."

"Might be some in the cupboard," Hank suggested.

Opening one door, washer and dryer; next door, mops and brooms; and door number three, boxed and canned goods. "Nope, no jam here," Lady reported. "Maybe the fridge?"

"No jam in there," Hank said. "I already looked, but there are two more closets over there."

Turning the knob of one door, Lady opened it to find a half bath and so went on to the next. "Hank, you need to look at this."

"Not sacrificing my hot breakfast," Hank stated. "Non-negotiable, and you shouldn't, either. Forget the jam and use butter."

"Have you looked in here?" Lady asked.

"I said no," Hank replied with impatience. "Your food will get cold and then you'll start complaining."

"We can eat later, Hank," Lady insisted. "There's a stairway leading down to a room that looks carpeted and plush, and it is not your typical basement."

Rolling his eyes, Hank grabbed a biscuit and headed over to see what the fuss was about. "This better be good because now I'm getting grumpy. I get grumpy when I don't keep my carbs up. Man, no rest for the weary or carb deficient."

"Stop complaining and go down there," Lady said, looking down the dark stairs. Blue darted past both of them and went down the stairs and disappeared. This surprised the two. Then Blue reappeared, barked, and disappeared again. "Well, now I have to go down there," Hank agreed. And down he went, turned to the right, and disappeared.

"Well, what is it?" Lady asked.

"Because you played the chicken, you've lost your cowgirl card!" Hank yelled. Muffled sounds could be heard from the basement, and Blue started barking frantically. More muffled sounds. Lady called out, "Come on, Hank, stop fooling around—you read about stuff like this!" Running to the broom closet Lady grabbed the first available makeshift weapon she could find—a mop. She hurried back to the basement door and called out, "I'm coming down there! And I want my cowgirl card back!"

Lights flashed off and on and Lady heard more muffled sounds and Blue continued to bark and growl. Down the steps Lady went, mop in hand, and turned the corner. Hank was seated comfortably in a wingback office chair and Blue was chewing on a tennis ball.

"What are you gonna do with that?" Hank teased. "Clean up the place? It looks pretty clean to me. Look at this place … I'd not be more surprised if …"

"I know," Lady said as she swatted him with the mop. "Save it … just save that awful analogy for the cowboy club."

Turning up the lights, Hank showed Lady what he had seen so far. "You're home, Sis … there's a baby grand in the other room and this right here appears to be a full-blown professional recording studio." He pointed to a cover that lay over the top of the control board. It was embroidered with Psalm 37:5: "COMMIT THY WAY UNTO THE LORD; TRUST ALSO IN HIM; AND HE SHALL BRING IT TO PASS."

"I don't ever have to go back to that City of Angels," Lady said with a laugh. "Ha! Not unless I want to. They can kiss my grits. Won't they be surprised!"

"As surprised as I may have been, if …" Hank said jokingly.

"Not that surprised," Lady said with a wink. "What would I do without you? Always with the jokes—thanks for being my bro."

"Glad to be a part of your life," Hank replied. "You take my mundane life and give it a little zip."

"My next effort to put some zip into someone's life is with a phone call," Lady said with a mischievous smile. "I'm going to call that no-good producer Harriman and demand that we finish the album project right here. He can also pack up my things and everything that is near and dear to me from out there and have it trucked right here to my new location."

"You need to call Momma, too," Hank suggested. "But first let's finish the breakfast—I don't get to cook very often, and I'd hate to see it go to waste."

Sitting down with phone in hand, Lady pressed the numbers while munching on Hank's homemade breakfast. "Hi, Momma ... I know, I know, but all this is so incredible and sad at the same time .... I do and I am taking my time, and with prayer ... I thank God for this opportunity that has been placed upon my table, tragic as it is .... No ... absolutely not, I am not going back there unless I am forced to. I can send for everything to be brought here. Harriman can come here, not that I want that man in my life—my contract does not say anything about where I record, only that it must be on time and mastered somewhere. Okay, you and Poppa need to come over here .... Yes, Hank and I have enough to eat .... Okay, Momma. ... Bye, and I love you, too."

Lady grabbed the last piece of cold toast from her plate and hung up the phone. Deep in thought, she went over to the window and looked down the lane. Tapping her foot for a moment, she went back to the phone and stared at it. Walking and munching around the table, walking and munching on the toast, she reached once again for the phone but hesitated. "Stop this crazy ritual and make the call!" Hank demanded.

"So what's the hurry—where are we going?" Lady asked.

"Crazy, Lady—and you are driving," Hank said with a laugh.

Smiling, Lady picked up the phone and said, "I have never met a man that I loathed so much but found so necessary to have around."

"Sounds like love to me," Hank observed. "Love, at times, is filled with contradictions."

"How would you know?" Lady asked. "You being the consummate bachelor."

"Have not been totally idle since you've been away, Sis," said Hank with a wink. "But some things are better kept close to the heart."

"Ha ha! Aren't you funny," Lady said with a smirk. Then she spoke into the phone. "Yes, operator, I'd like to make a collect call to 555-777-4444, and please tell whoever answers that it is collect from Lady Parsons," Lady winked at Hank.

Hank just shook his head and said, "More sand for the man."

On the other end, Lady could hear the ringing and finally a female with a foreign accent answered, "Hello."

The call was accepted, and Lady spoke. "Hello, yes hello, this is Lady, and who in the world is this? ... Oh yes, of course, Maria. Put Harriman on the phone, please." Lady put her hand on the receiver, looked at Hank, and said, "That no-good is still in bed."

Going back to listening, Lady could hear shuffling and movement and the passing of the phone. "Lady, is that you?"

"No joke, Mr. Slick," Lady answered. "Where are you, Harriman, and what are you doing?"

"I'm in bed, half asleep. Thought you weren't coming back until Friday. Are you downstairs, or what—in town?" was Harriman's response.

"Who answered the phone, Slick?" Lady asked peevishly.

"What the heck, that was Maria," Harriman replied. "I left the phone on the dining table. What's the matter with you? What is your problem—no, hey, I am sorry. I guess you are still grieving and you know I am sorry for your loss."

"Nothing, Harriman, nothing's wrong, and thanks for your concern," Lady responded. "Here is the deal now, and it's a game changer, so hang on to your silk nightie. I wanted to let you know I'm not coming back on Friday, or any time soon. I am sending for everything that is near and dear to me, if you catch my meaning. We will be recording in my new studio here in Texas. Make plans to come here to finish the recording, and if you want, you can bring Joey the engineer—I like him; and I will call Will myself!" Lady immediately hung up the phone, not giving Harriman time to respond.

Giving Lady a thumbs up, Hank snickered. Then the phone came alive. Lady motioned for Hank to answer it. "Parsons residence ... and who should I say is calling? ... Oh, Mr. Harriman ... let me see if she's available; she has a very busy schedule."

"Hello," Lady said slowly, "Harriman, honey, is that you?"

"You know perfectly well it is," Harriman said, a little put off. "You can't just demand how and where we conduct business. You are a thousand miles away from where the action is. You are out of touch with reality. Besides, how do we know your place is state of the art? And now, while I am awake, who answered your phone, and why should I care?"

"My brother, and to answer your state-of-the-art question," Lady said smugly, "I should know and you shouldn't have to ask, but it is top notch, has a grand piano and I have all the musicians I need. I'll call Scottie and his boys will be here in a flash—hearing me?"

"We will see ... we will see," Harriman answered. "I'll fly out to no man's land on Monday next week, and we'll see then if your ducks are in a row. If so, then you can send for your things. You are one tough nut is all I have to say, and full of surprises, to boot."

"You didn't even ask about the funeral, or if I'm okay," Lady said.

"You didn't give me the chance," Harriman replied.

"No, guess I didn't," Lady agreed.

"So how have you come by all this new-found independence?" Harriman asked.

"Jesse, apparently, was more than I could have imagined," Lady answered. "Sadly, by this tragedy he left me all he had claimed on this earth, and more. Where I am living now is within his legacy."

"Sounds like you are queen of the mountain," Harriman observed.

"Literally, and I have an obligation now to pay forward what I've been given," Lady said. "I cannot and will not take this responsibility lightly."

"I feel what you are telling me, and I will make flight arrangements today," Harriman affirmed. "Will you, or can you, have someone pick me up at the airport?"

"Of course, just let me know time and flight," Lady said. "I will call Will and have him fly with Joey. Of course, they fly and you buy."

"Don't I always, and I hope my cell works out there is all I can say," Harriman snapped.

"Okay, Harriman." Lady hung up the phone.

AFFIRMATION AND DISCOVERY

Standing attentively and holding a sign with *Harriman* written on it, Hank watched the passengers coming off the puddle jumper that carried passengers from larger facilities to the small county airport. There were no overhead announcements, just a small board showing flight numbers and arrivals and departures. Hank wondered about the man. His sister had spoken about him with so much apprehension and disdain. Maybe this guy will be wearing a silk suit, Italian leather shoes, designer shades, and an expensive watch. After all, this clown is supposed to be a big-time producer, and coming from Hollywood, what can you expect?

"Looking for me?" Harriman asked as he tapped Hank on the shoulder.

Hank turned around to greet a tall, lanky, not bad-looking fellow in a baseball cap, tropical shirt, and blue jeans. *Pretty normal*, Hank thought as he said, "If you be Harriman, I guess you are my passenger. Good to meet ya—I am Hank, Lady's brother and your chauffeur. Do you have all your bags?"

"I do," Harriman confirmed and then said, "There is something I must take care of before we leave, so please give me a few minutes and please watch my bags. I'll be right back."

Watching Harriman, Hank noticed that he went over to where a young Latina woman was seated next to a little boy. Harriman was giving her some money and they chatted for about five minutes. When Harriman returned, Hank asked, "Is that woman a friend of yours? Does she need a ride?"

Smiling, Harriman answered, "Oh, she and that little boy were seated next to me on the flight and I decided to help them out and find them a place to stay while they were visiting—they're nice people, and now they're good to go."

"That's very kind of you," Hank observed, smiling as he grabbed one of the man's bags. "Hope you don't mind riding in a pick-up truck. It ain't pretty, but it gets the job done."

"What makes you think that I would?" Harriman asked.

"Oh, I don't know;" Hank replied, "being where you're from lends an impression."

"Most people out there are from somewhere else," Harriman explained, "and I'm no different. I grew up on a vegetable farm in Oregon. So I am used to a pick-up truck—and manure, too. Small beginnings Hank, small beginnings."

"I see," said Hank. He thought that this guy didn't seem so out of touch. Putting Harriman's bags in the truck bed, Hank offered, "You want something to eat?" Then he hesitated for a moment and asked, "Are you vegetarian or vegan?"

Grinning, Harriman replied, "I'm not as fussy as Lady, so anything at this point will do."

"Cool," Hank said. He thought that he seemed to take a liking to this producer guy, but all the votes weren't in just yet. "Burgers okay?"

"Whatever," Harriman answered.

Pulling into a fast-food place, the very one that he took Lady to on the day of her arrival, Hank asked, "You want to sit, or take out?"

"Let's eat in," Harriman replied. "I think you and I need to talk for a few minutes and relax."

A little curious now, Hank said, "That works for me."

Once seated at a table, Harriman began to unwrap his meal and ask the obvious, "So you are Lady's twin brother?"

"Yessir, I am," Hank answered while taking a bite of french fries.

"I see the resemblance," Harriman remarked and then opened up. "Lady's a talent, Hank, and that's for sure. I don't know what she has told you or not about this insane business we are in. It has never been a smooth path between the creative aspects and the business of getting it done. She looks at me sometimes as a contentious adversary. Don't get me wrong, business is business and time is money and timing here is everything. Lady is the commodity, and as a company we have to protect the investment.

"As cold-hearted as all that sounds, on the other side of the coin, I truly have her best interest at heart. She has journeyed a hard road, Hank, and paid her dues in the process. Some came by her own decisions, and others through no fault of her own. Life just happens, as in the case of the tragedy that has brought us here today."

Amazed by the opening monologue, Hank continued to eat as he listened, nodding here and there. When Harriman finished, Hank put down his burger and shook his hand and said, "You know I was worried. I thought you'd be some high-minded thought-he-knew-it-all. But you seem down to earth, and seem to be looking out for my sister ... and don't take this the wrong way—you gotta look out for you, too, and I understand that."

"Aha, so it is good we are having this conversation. Get things out in the open. Find out the intentions of this city dweller," Harriman noted. "That's fair enough. But life does hold surprises."

"How so?" Hank inquired.

"All in good time, Hank," Harriman replied. "And it is all good, I assure you."

"Cool," Hank said. "Ready to roll?"

"Let's hit it," Harriman answered. "I can't wait to see Lady's new digs."

"Oh, now that's the story," Hank stated. "You will be impressed."

As they drove down the highway, they made idle chit chat. Harriman told Hank how and where he had grown up. "I was the elder of two boys growing up on a small farm and always wanted to leave that place," Harriman told him. "Could not stand to be there in the middle of nowhere, as I believed it to be. So once I was out of high school, I headed for the city—not LA at first, but Seattle. I earned my degree as an attorney, and I saw there were many opportunities in Seattle for musicians. But I saw them getting taken over by the clubs and various music venues. I decided to get them organized, and soon they were earning better money because we set standards for fair pay. Because of that, I helped many individuals and groups get ahead and receive recording contracts. My name got around and soon I found myself getting off a bus in LA. After building up some seed money for my new vegetable garden, so to speak, I started to produce those who I felt had a chance at making it to the big show."

"That's where and when you met my sister?" Hank asked.

"Yes, and when I first met her, she was ... let's say, a mess," Harriman said. "Lady was in a bad way emotionally, just about bankrupt and didn't know which way to turn. She had been done over by people who did not hold her best interests at heart, and I saw how they took advantage of her. So we sued them and won."

"Wow, so you really helped her out," Hank said, shaking his head in approval and offering, "Let me show you where Lady and I grew up—it's on the way."

"Sure," Harriman agreed, "that'd be great; but let's pull over and hold up for a moment," Harriman asked, taking a deep breath.

"Sure, Mr. Harriman," Hank agreed and pulled the truck to the side of the road. "What's up?"

Harriman paused, in thought. "Hank, I like you and I place you in my trust. There is much to be done today, but first I must lay this all out before we get to Lady."

With his interest peaked and his guard up, Hank wondered what was coming. It was serious, he could sense the intent. Would this be a confession?

"Hank," Harriman looked directly at him, "I don't know how to do this other than be right down the center lane. Your sister, Lady, is my client. Being her advisor and confidant, I must tell you this in order to move forward. I cannot do what is best for her without bringing you into the inner circle of confidence."

"This sounds too serious," Hank stated. "But continue, even though I am not so sure I want to hear this."

"I know, but this needs to come out, and trust me, I am stepping all over attorney-client privilege," Harriman said. "So here goes. When Lady first came to LA, she was carrying a load of talent with her and also, unbeknown to her … "

Immediately Hank cut him off. "I knew it, Mr. Harriman. I knew it not just because of things she said, but even more from what she didn't say. Even Jesse was suspicious. But I have to ask why … why didn't she own up to it? That borders on being cruel … not that I am judging, I won't do that. She must have had reasons, even though they be unreasonable."

"Reasoning this all out, perhaps *rationalizing* is a better word," Harriman put up his hands. "I don't know. Pride, perhaps, being caught up in the pending success and all of a sudden there appears this huge responsibility. Hank, she hid it well. Don't get it wrong, she was very careful with her diet, did not expose herself to extremes at that time. Not like later, can't speak for that."

"But how did she keep this from fans or the press snoops?" Hank questioned.

"Mexico," Harriman answered.

"At the airport?" Hank asked, and quickly stated, "That's her nanny, and that was her son."

"Dude," Harriman observed, "you should be a detective."

"I'm on board with all of this," Hank said with a tear.

"You okay, Hank?" Harriman gently asked and said, "I know this is a lot to take in …."

"No, no I am fine," Hank said. "Maybe it is a tear for Jesse, maybe it is a tear for her not trusting her family. Not trusting us enough. For her to think that we wouldn't understand … well, that is ridiculous. Then again comes the benefit of the doubt … wasn't there standing in her shoes. Mexico …?

"Yes, we packed Lady off on a private jet in the dark of night, Hank," Harriman explained. "While there, she met Maria and loved her manners. Maria had been an EVAC nurse for the army and wanted to come to America. Lady, being the kind soul she is, took it to heart and provided the means. Maria became invaluable not only to Lady but also to the whole complex we live in. That's the Lady-baby-Maria story. And here we are today. You got a CDL—can you drive a tractor trailer?"

Deep in thought, Hank sat for a moment. "CDL … sure, I can do that. Part of future plans, Mr. Harriman? In the dark of night?"

Harriman smiled at Hank's wit. "Sorta—daylight recon is more like it—sneaky under the picket wire and return without notice."

"I can accomplish that," Hank assured. "I know the rumors are going to come—personally I can handle that—and they will flow fast and nasty. Just as at the funeral people wore two faces, and as Lady said then that she forgave them, so do I. There's a saying that until you walk a mile in another man's shoes you have no right to judge, and that applies here. The people my heart breaks for are Momma and Poppa. I am concerned for them, Mr Harriman, and how they will handle all this."

"We will leave that work up to Lady," Harriman advised.

Viewing the expanse of the ranch from the truck window, Harriman whistled approvingly and said, "You and your folks do a bit of work each and every day. It takes a lot of effort to keep this place up and running. I can tell that your pride is in each and every corner of this land. Well done, Hank."

"Thank you, Mr. Harriman," Hank said, pleased at the compliment. "Now I will take you to Lady's new home."

As they drove up the narrow, winding road, Harriman said, "Now this seems different for Texas."

"It's one of the few places where there are hills like this. We are getting closer to Arkansas, which has more rolling hills and mountains," Hank explained.

"The tall pines are beautiful," Harriman observed.

As they approached the house that Jesse built, again Harriman gave a whistle and said, "Lady is one blessed person. She will be hard pressed to ever want to leave this. WOW! In fact, I am not sure that I want to go back to LA. This seems like a permanent vacation."

"You ain't seen nothing yet, Mr. Harriman," Hank declared. "This is just the tip of the iceberg."

Lady appeared on the porch with Blue, who immediately started barking. "Friend, or foe?" Lady shouted, looking at Harriman.

Harriman looked up, held up his hands, and shouted back, "Friend for sure, friend for life! How could I not be, in such a tranquil and beautiful setting? We should do a movie or video shoot here, how could we not?"

"Stop with the business first routine," Lady requested with a grin. "Grab your gear and come inside. Where's the rest of the crew—Will and Joey the engineer?"

"They're on the way," Harriman explained. "They had to catch a later flight, but I wanted to come ahead, anyway."

Hank already had Harriman's bags in hand and led the way up the stairs. Upon reaching the top, Harriman gave Lady a hug and said, "I am so glad to see you, Lady. Most of all, I am glad we are on a better and more friendly communication level today." Harriman pulled away and waved his hand towards the verdant vista that he witnessed from the porch and said, "How could you not be, with all this going on. Wow—I say again—wow!"

"I know, Harriman, I know," Lady said sheepishly as a tear flowed down her cheek. "It has been a lesson in paradox, Harriman. This all came with such a price."

> **"**
> "I know," Lady said sheepishly as a tear flowed down her cheek. "It has been a lesson in paradox, Harriman. This all came with such a price."
> **"**

Harriman couldn't help himself and gave Lady another hug and said, with understanding, "I know it did, Lady. And I know I cannot give an accounting for what you must be feeling and going through. I am truly sorry for your loss."

"Thank you, Harriman," Lady said quietly. "Thank you."

Lady wiped the tear and said, "Enough of this melancholy. Let's have some lunch."

"Really, you?" Hank questioned.

Harriman looked puzzled, first gazing at Hank and then at Lady.

This scrutiny gave Lady time to pause, and she quickly came to a conclusion. "Quiet, Hank," Lady blurted out. "Harriman, Hank ... you guys don't think I can prepare a meal, do you? Both of you get inside before I feed it to Blue. You guys better not have stopped to get anything to eat."

Turning and gazing at their faces as she walked, Lady didn't notice any incriminating food particles dangling from their faces, so she said, "You guys both look pretty dumb and numb at that question, so I'll give you the benefit of the doubt. And yes, the array of food is healthy—very California for Mr. LA. Fruits, nuts, vegetables; and the pancakes and spreads are GMO free."

"Well, you used to live in LA, and from what I recall, you were vegan at that time," Harriman stated.

"Hey, Harriman, in case you hadn't noticed, you have crossed over the border and entered the Republic of Texas, and me being a Texican, I am trying my best to remain vege-tar-i-an out here in cattle country USA. Believe me when I say that when I look at a cow right now, my mouth waters and I see all the prime cuts laid out like a road map on that cows' hide—shoulder cuts to rib eye and sirloin."

Laughing at Lady's joke, Hank put down Harriman's bags and moved toward the food. Harriman picked up a few sprigs of celery and some carrots and dips and began to nosh. "Good ranch dressing. You added some heat and that's great, very southwestern of you."

"Well thank you, Harriman," Lady replied. "Thanks for noticing, and for the culinary critique."

"Credit where it's due, my Lady," Harriman said, saluting with a carrot slathered in dressing.

"I'll take Harriman's bags to the guest room and then I've got to get going," Hank stated.

"Where are you going in such a hurry?" Lady asked.

Just then, several vehicles pulled up outside and Lady went to the window to look. "It's Will and Joey!"

"Yup, right on time," Harriman quipped. "Love it when a plan comes together. Looks like we'll get some studio time in today, if you're up for it?"

Hank scurried past Lady on his way out the door. "'Scuse me, see ya later, Sis ... be back before dark!"

Will and Joey came in as Hank left, saying, "Hi, ya'll and bye y'all, by the way I'm Hank, Lady's brother." They shook hands and Hank quickly took off in his pick-up, leaving a dust trail down the driveway.

"Yup, that's my crazy twin brother, Hank," Lady explained. "Don't know where he's goin', just know he can't be late."

Laughing, Will and Joey hugged Lady and she said, "Welcome, fellas, to my new home; there's food on the table."

"If you don't mind, Lady, we will surely take you up on that offer," said Will, eagerly rubbing his hands together.

"Yeah, they don't give you nuthin' on the plane anymore unless you pre-pay with a credit card, like at the pumps when you gas up the car," added Joey. "I'm starvin' Marvin right now!"

"Well have at it, boys," Harriman said with approval, "and check out the spiced ranch dressing. It appears to be another one of Lady's originals. When we are done feeding our faces, we will check out Lady's 'state of the art' studio."

"Watch it, Harriman," Lady warned.

"Just repeating what you said," Harriman sheepishly confirmed.

Between bites, Will said, "Don't worry Lady—I'm sure it will do just fine."

"Not to worry, Lady," Joey added. "If it's anything like your dressing invention it will be spot on."

"I'm not worried, guys," Lady assured them. "Harriman is sometimes like sand in the swimming attire."

Saluting, Harriman said, "No matter what I do or say ... Lady ... you are the best of the tests."

"What do you say guys, now that you are fed, we check out the studio," Lady invited. She opened what appeared to them as a closet door, and they all followed her down the stairs.

"How novel, a below-ground studio," Harriman mumbled. "How do you get all the instruments with the players down here?"

"Harriman," Lady said, "I can feel and hear your unwarranted negativity."

After reaching the bottom, they all turned right and Joey assured Harriman, "She's right—STATE OF THE ART—for sure."

Looking through the control room window into the sound booth, Will asked, "State of the art to be sure, but how in the world did you get the grand piano in here?"

"Because Mr. Harriman was so concerned as to access and egress I will explain," Lady replied. "Joey, push that button on the wall, *room access*."

There was a whirring sound, and as all looked into the sound booth, the right wall began to move. Apparently, part of it was on tracks, and an eight-foot section opened and slid like a parlor door into the wall.

"Question answered," Lady stated, pleased with herself. "And there is a storage room behind the wall for equipment and extra gear. Jesse thought of everything."

> "
> It is up to you and us to move forward this legacy that he has so thoughtfully placed in your capable hands.
> "

Will spoke first. "I can say for all of us here standing in your studio, Lady, that we wish we had personally met Jesse. We all know how much he meant to you and we can see just how generous of an individual he was. He had your best interest at heart. It is up to you and us to move forward this legacy that he has so thoughtfully placed in your capable hands. Let us not waste it, for that would be a sin."

Gently touching Will's face, Lady said, "Those are such kind and challenging words, Will, and they have not fallen on deaf ears."

"Joey," Harriman said, "You heard the Lady. Do you have the goods? And if so, let's complete this project."

"Sir, yes sir, in the car, sir," Joey answered.

"Well, get to it and retrieve," Harriman commanded.

Turning on his heel, Joey ran up the stairs.

There was a new look of confidence in Lady's eyes as she nodded her head, looking first at Will and then at Harriman. Opening the door to the sound booth where the piano was, she asked Will to follow her. She said to Harriman, "There's a big comfy chair just like the ones you are used to in those highfalutin, hi-priced studios out there in tinsel town. You can have a sit in this low-budget place—I'm sure your butt'l fit in this one, too."

"This one's better ...," Harriman was cut off by the closing of the double sound-room door before he could get another word in. And whoosh, Joey was back in a flash. "What's the matter, Harriman?" Joey asked as he opened the protective metal box of the tool kit.

"Nothing, Joey," Harriman said. "I try to understand, but ..."

"She's gone through, and is still going through, some real-life drama," Joey contended. "Give some room and try not to be so ... what is the word I am looking for?"

"Smug, sarcastic, judgmental, condescending," Harriman listed.

"Yeah, all of the above," Joey said with a chuckle. "Even though Lady does have a prima-donna-diva complex sometimes." They both laughed.

Seated at the piano with Lady, Will said, "Ya know, you could go a little easier on that fella. If you count up all the good things he has done for you, Lady, I'd say they far outweigh the bad. What'dya think about that?"

Picking at some notes and chords on the piano, Lady answered, "Yes, I've been thinkin' on that matter. And it's been leanin' pretty heavily on me Will, ... just that ... what really matters in life is a question. Ya know what, Will?"

"What, Lady?" Will said.

"I'm not afraid of dying," Lady stated.

"WHAT are you telling me?" Will asked.

"I have come full circle now," Lady answered. "I had been so lost in the dust of a race that I was trying to win. Going round and round, caught, like in one of those revolving doors, not knowing when to jump out, blinded, not knowing that I had already won. I was never satisfied, could never enjoy what I had already accomplished. I was always searching for something to leave behind that held value, like receiving accolades from my peers. As if that really matters. Now I'm satisfied; not afraid to die to the world, Will. I am at peace within my Lord and Savior Jesus Christ."

"Those are some really personal observations—thank you for sharing them," Will responded. Not knowing exactly how to take what Lady had just confided in him, he cautiously added, "You still have much to contribute to this world. There is a fountain of good in you and you have many who look up to you for love, understanding, and the sharing of your experiences of life. All these things hold value to those who are coming after you. That is also part of your legacy—the sharing of what you know to be true. Just like you have done with me, share this with the world, even if they don't want to hear it; tell your story and plant the seeds of truth."

> *That is also part of your legacy — the sharing of what you know to be true. Just like you have done with me, share this with the world, even if they don't want to hear it; tell your story and plant the seeds of truth.*

Breaking through the thoughtful conversation was Joey's voice over the intercom. "Are you guys ready to get on with the production? Aahh, wait a minute—Harriman wants to say something."

"Lady, can you and Will please come to the engineer's booth for a minute?" Harriman asked.

Entering the booth, Lady asked Harriman, "What's up?"

"I have been sitting here as I always do, playing with my cell phone as I listen to song after song being played and worked on. But not today," Harriman said. "My cell phone doesn't work out here and we have not started production yet and I am getting stressed. But ya know what? Not today! Right here and now I want to reaffirm in ... no I need reaffirmation. After hearing Lady's song and the story that goes along with it, I realize that I am off the rails about my purpose here; I am a devout hypocrite at this point, and I am sick of me. And Lady, you are so right."

"About what?" Lady asked. "Is this about wasting time? But oh, this is my place, my dime now, isn't it?"

"This is not about tit for tat," Harriman said. "I get it, I was a tightwad back there and I am sorry."

"A tightwad and then some," Lady said with a smirk. "But you are repenting now, is that it?"

"Give me some slack here," Harriman pleaded. "We need to admit when enough is enough."

"Yes, we do," Lady agreed. "And is today the day?"

"Lady, let the man speak," Will prompted. "I believe him to be serious—he's telling the truth."

"Like how can you tell when a lawyer is lying, kinda truth?" Lady asked smugly.

Chuckles could be heard from Joey and Will, and Harriman said with a smile, "Yes, Lady, you have me there, as I am a prestigious member of the bar association in California. But what I am expressing is real. What I am saying is to leave our lives in God's hands. Time is a gift, a very precious commodity, as it is all we have. Our responsibility … is our ability deemed by how we spend it."

"Why, Simon Harriman, why choose right here and now to come out and say … HALLELUJAH?" Lady asked.

> **"**
> *Time is a gift, a very precious commodity, as it is all we have. Our responsibility … is our ability deemed by how we spend it.*
> **"**

As Joey and Will kept watching the conversation, their heads pinged back and forth like the audience at a tennis match.

"Oh, don't get used to it, mister, or go getting all mushy on me," Lady quipped.

"Okay, this is good," Harriman observed. "We're working out all the pent-up frustrations from the past. I am totally for that."

"This is the first time I have experienced or seen a resemblance of anything human coming from you," Lady said, almost sanctimoniously.

Ping, back to Harriman: "You will see more of that side come out of me from now on, I promise."

Pong, back to Lady: "Don't go making a promise you can't keep, Simon."

"Okay, okay, but seriously now, can we all take a knee, because I have something that I need to share," Simon asked humbly.

Adding to the request, Joey said, "I think I need to do this, as well."

Jumping in, Will said, "Maybe Lady should lead us in. She has brought it all together here today. Let's ask God to lead us the rest of the way."

"You know what, Will," Lady said, "I defer to Simon today as he seems in the Holy Spirit at this time. I think we should let him lead. Simon …."

Taking a knee, Simon prayed, "Dear Lord, our Heavenly Father, in your Son's precious name Jesus Christ, I ask for forgiveness for myself. I have been lost, but have been found by these wonderful people who I am surrounded by today. I thank You for guiding me here, and I ask a special blessing upon this house and studio and all who may enter. I thank you for the privilege to serve, and ask you to bless this upcoming concert which, until this moment, Lady had no idea of its existence. I ask to bring all who are able, to come here to hear a special dedication of Lady's sanctuary. This is a place where all may be welcome and find a safe haven. Father God, anoint and bless this place in the holy name of Your Son, Jesus Christ. We ask that Your will, Heavenly Father, be done. Amen."

They got up from bent knees, and there were sounds. Sounds like a train approaching outside, the rumbling of tractor-trailers, suddenly the barking of Blue, and the air horn of a truck announced their arrival.

"That train sound," Lady said, laughing. "Slo' Hand Scottie and The Trainwreck Survivors—they're here, too?"

"Called them in on this deal myself," Harriman said. "And their promoter and manager, Brad Hastings."

"What have you done, Simon, that I know nothing about?" Lady accused. "Are you—you can't be serious, Simon Harriman. I want to know who all are involved in this scheme. I want names, even though the list may be long!"

All eyes fell upon Simon, who was all smiles as he explained, "Oh, I am not the only one at fault here. The perp list is long and circuitous and leads through family and friends. If you think that Scottie and the 'Survivor' boys are not friends who would want to be a part of this celebration—you don't know them at all. This is about your celebration of a new life. You are thanking all who have taken a part in bringing you to where you are today.

"Oh, your brother who was honking the horn, for sure," Simon continued. "He let me know that all the crew for the stage and lighting and sound had arrived to put on a full-blown concert. Flyers, newspaper ads, radio, TV—now I'd guess for sure this show will go on. You have the best backup musicians. Who knows your music and style better than Scottie and the Survivors? Best warm up bands you can imagine. They have donated their time and energy to give you a leg up."

"It's not all donated, Simon; who is paying what needs to be paid?" Lady questioned.

"We are asking for donations," Simon answered. "I will donate whatever is needed, over and above. This is a gift from me to you, to kick off the next phase of your career—whatever you choose that to be."

"DISCOVERY OF TRUTH" CONCERT

Looking out from stage right, Lady stood with Will, her music coordinator. "It's gonna be okay, Lady. We've rehearsed for the past week."

Slo' Hand Scottie and The Trainwreck Survivors were standing ready. Scottie came over and said to Lady, "Put the worry button on pause. The boys and I and you are coming out and will surpass by far anything that we have ever done before."

"All the bands playing before us are so good," Lady said, with concern.

"They're not you," Scottie stated. "That's why the people are here. You are the drawing card."

"Yes, what Scottie said—these people are here to see you, Lady," Will said, trying to lift Lady's confidence. "Stop this self-doubt that someone else has whispered in your ear. Place this and everything you do in the Lord's hands. Isn't that what Simon prayed for? Isn't that what you told me, Lady? Claim it!"

"Amen, Will." Lady continued, "There's an ocean of faces out there, that's for certain. Where's that sneaky Simon?"

"He went with Hank to pick up your parents," Will stated while checking the time. "He should have been here by now. You're on in about twenty. But this band might get an encore."

Lady gave Will a sidelong look of concern.

"Stop it," Will said warning sternly, shaking a finger at her.

"Oh look, there's Mom and Dad," Lady said excitedly. "Hank's brought them in, and they've never heard me play and sing live in concert since the first concert at the fair way back when. Will, this is so special. Oh my, and there are the busybody ladies, too. They just had to come see, so they could say they came and saw. What a variety of people are here tonight!"

"Standing room only," Will said. "Bring your own seat or sit on the grass."

Scottie and the Survivors came over and got ready. They waited patiently as the warm-up band left the stage and the roadies cleared and reset. Lady, Will, and the band held hands as she led them in prayer. Then it was time. Scottie and the Survivors quickly took their positions. Tonight there was no sound of a train, no whistle or venting steam. It was the presence of Lady, who moved as a professional always does—with humility she crossed to center and stood before the audience. The crowd stood up and applauded, for it was her they came to see. Now it was Lady's turn to speak.

"I want to thank everyone here for coming tonight. It has been a journey that has brought me full circle—home again—and this time, for good. I owe so many people so much for this special life I have led. You, the people of this community, I know have shared my pain as we recently lost our dear brother Jesse. And Jesse always reminded me that only here but by the grace of God go I, and I will include all of us in this matter, and I am here only because God has led me.

"The good Lord has looked down upon me with compassion. He sees us all not as others see us, not as we see ourselves, and not as we have been, but rather, He sees us in the light of what we may become.

"I believe that we live two lives while here on earth; the one we experience and learn with—and the second, what we do with that knowledge once it is acquired. Some folks will accept it and pay it forward. Others will hide their newly found light, and sadly, there are the ones who just don't get it.

> **"**
> It has taken years of living in fear, a river of unending tears, but today, yes, I am still a work in progress, a survivor if you will, but I place all in His hands, the only one capable of my deliverance — my Savior, Jesus Christ.
> **"**

"It has taken me a while, but now I get it. It has taken years of living in fear, a river of unending tears, but today, yes, I am still a work in progress, a survivor if you will, but I place all in His hands, the only one capable of my deliverance—my Savior, Jesus Christ. Amen!"

"*Amen*" could be heard reverberating throughout the crowd.

"The song I am about to play, I wrote for Jesse. In a letter he wrote to me he requested that it be dedicated not to him, but to our Lord and Savior, Jesus Christ. I have done as requested, and every concert played, every note played, and every word sung here and ever after is praise to the promise that Jesus made to you and to me. So the title of the song is just that—'The Promise.'"

A friend—they called me—said
"The life I lead is killing me."
"You know," I told my friend,
"I've got something that you need."

When you need protection
From all the trouble in your soul,
Read the truth, find peace of mind,
In the greatest story ever told.

CHORUS
And you know—if you need a friend,
And you know—come take His hand—He'll be your friend.

Within the darkest hours
His light stands burning bright;
Read line by line and verse by verse;
The truth will get you through this fight.

Don't let the daily burden
Of this life weigh you down.
Plant your feet up on the rock
Where love and strength abound.

CHORUS

And time—it comes to pass by
As it does for all worldly things.
Open up your heart, you'll surely find
The peace and joy that lies within.

Christ is the answer;
In His promise we must believe.
We are saved by grace, show your faith;
Through your prayer he intercedes.

CHORUS and FINISH

At the conclusion of the song, you could have heard a pin drop on the grass, but suddenly requests started coming, out of the depth of reverence and solitude. People must have pondered the message delivered, and as the calls of *"amen"* began, a wave of bodies stood up on their feet. It was as if the Holy Ghost lifted all, and a call for a second playing of the song went out. Lady became emotional over the song's acceptance. The musicians took the call, and the song was revisited.

The concert went forward, and they played other songs that Lady had written over the years. She shared the success with Slo' Hand Scottie, playing some of his tunes, as well. Later she would recall that never had she experienced an encore after the very first song of a concert.

Standing on stage right, Simon Harriman, Lady's producer and confidant, was all smiles. Lady, of course, received another encore, and of course, they again played "The Promise."

Coming off the stage, Simon shook the musician's hands and gave Lady a huge hug as he handed her roses. "For me?" Lady humbly accepted. She quickly asked, "Are Mom and Dad coming back here? Did Hank go and fetch them outta the crowd?"

"Don't worry, Lady," Simon assured her, "they'll be here any second."

Just then, Lady's mother and father and Hank, holding Blue on a leash, appeared.

Lady was beside herself in tears. "Oh Mom, Dad, I am so happy you are here at last to see a real concert."

"It was wonderful, darling, and that song…" Lady's mother commented, shaking her head.

"I'd put my money on that horse as a winner," Lady's father remarked. "Come here for hugs all around." Lady fell into her parents' arms.

Pulling away, wiping tears from her eyes, gaining composure, Lady took a deep breath and said, "Mom, Dad, Hank, there is someone I want you to meet."

The three of Lady's family now looked at her with curiosity. "What's the matter, dear?" her mother asked, noticing that Lady was a little nervous.

"Have you run off and gotten married since last we spoke?" her father asked.

Chuckling at her father's question, Lady replied, a little embarrassed, "No, of course not!"

And then from behind Simon Harriman, a lady named Maria appeared, holding a little boy's hand. He broke free and rushed to give Lady a hug as he asked, "Momma, what's wrong—why are you crying—it was a really good concert, wasn't it?"

Lady scooped him up and presented her son to the family, "Mom, Dad, Hank, I want you to meet my son, your grandson, and Hank, your nephew, Jesse Junior."

"Oh!" Momma shouted, clapping her hands. "Ain't no denying that one being Jesse Junior, the spittin' image!"

"Well I'll be, make me a talking horse!" Poppa exclaimed.

Hank stood silent at first, nodded his head, and pointed both his pointer fingers at his sister. "I knew it, Sis, as God is my witness and He made little green apples. I wasn't one hundred percent sure, but I sensed something was up!"

Not one for shyness, Hank suddenly went into animation mode slapping his thigh and shouting, "Well, hee-haw, little nephew ... welcome to Texas!" Hank ran over and ruffled Jesse Junior's hair, shook his little hand and said, "You and me, son, are gonna be bestest pards. We'll have tons of fun, and that's for Texas certain!"

Looking at his mother, little Jesse asked, "Is he crazy, Momma?"

"Oh yes, Jesse, and that's one certifiable crazy Texan uncle you have there," Lady assured him.

"Now later we want the whole story, and nothing left out, young lady," her father requested. He shook little Jesse's hand. "Welcome home, little fella."

Father's request was reiterated by Momma. "Nothin' left out, you hear me, Lady? You got some explaining to do! I want the truth, the whole truth, and nothing but the truth," as she pointed a finger her way.

"So help me, God and my attorney, Jesus, will be there with me to advise, as I can neither confirm nor deny anything without Him interceding for me," Lady said with a smile as they went to the house for a smorgasbord, Texas style.

Or is that plant-based Texan fare? Whatever, they happily gathered together, giving thanks and praise for all they had been blessed with.

AFTERWORD

But Godliness with contentment is great gain. For we brought nothing into this world, and it is certain we can carry nothing out. And with having food and raiment let us be therewith content. But they that will be rich fall into temptation and a snare, and into many foolish and hurtful lusts, which drown men in destruction and perdition. For the love of money is the root of all evil: which while some coveted after, they have erred from the faith, and pierced themselves through with many sorrows. But thou, O man of God, flee these things; and follow after righteousness, godliness, faith, love, patience, meekness. Fight the good fight of faith, lay hold on eternal life, whereunto thou art also called, and hast professed a good profession before many witnesses. (1 Timothy 6:6–12)

It is not the things that we acquire in life that become the problem. God desires that we have a full and abundant life. Rather, it is our intent of use; it is stewardship of that which we have been given. It is written in Malachi 3:10, "Bring ye all the tithes into the storehouse, that there may be meat in mine house, and prove me now herewith, saith the LORD of hosts, if I will not open you the windows of heaven, and pour you out a blessing, that there shall not be room enough to receive it."

Almost everyone who comes to church has been suspicious of the collection plate at one time or another, and questions as to where and how the offerings are used. We are inundated by ministers and evangelists on the TV asking for support of this cause or that ministry. The public has become jaded by the bling pastors who certainly have more than they need, and have misappropriated vast amounts of wealth. The thought of supporting yet another cause becomes a task filled with trepidation.

But remember, when you are returning a portion of God's goodness, which has graciously been given to you, you are giving back to God what is rightfully His. If your intent is righteous, God knows your heart. But if the company or persons you give the tithe, donation, or gift to, misuse the appropriations, now it falls on their heads and the good Lord surely knows their hearts and their intentions.

The greatest commodity that has been gifted us is time. But how do we spend it? With whom do you spend it? How much time do you dedicate to sharing with your children, parents, spouse, education, internet, TV, and the newest provocateur in the misuse of time, the mobile phone? Ooops, I almost forgot about God! Daily devotion should be at the top of the list.

Perhaps there is a bad habit you have; replace it with a better habit—in service to others, perhaps? Most times those temptations, whatever they are, come about when you are totally alone and most vulnerable. When you feel that attraction coming on, pick up the Bible, and maybe a devotional or prayer-study guide; but first pray for guidance, and you will receive it. Each time Satan tempted Jesus Christ in the wilderness, Jesus simply replied, "For it is written, do not tempt the Lord thy God." So the next time you are tempted, immerse yourself in God's Holy Word and say, "Get thee behind me, Satan."

Prayer is a spiritual muscle of immeasurable value, which only gets stronger and stronger the more you use it. Remember, all it requires is a little of your time each day. God's communication network is constant, never busy, no black outs, no dropped calls, and you can transmit and receive from anywhere in the universe. Best of all, it's free—won't cost you one thin dime—only an investment of time, and time well spent. Blessings to you. May God fulfill your deepest desires of life; let His will be done.

As mentioned in the Dedication, you can hear the song, "The Promise," on YouTube, performed by Shana Saint, by going to https://1ref.us/23k.

To read True Events Behind the Song: "The Promise" visit https://1ref.us/promise.

The Gift

Words and music by Benjamin K. Bachman
Copyright 2008 Produced by Larry B. Bachman
Vocals: Benjamin K. Bachman
Keyboards: Andrew Frye
Strings: Milo Deering
Percussion: Eric Sipe

A little boy goes running by …
He trips and scrapes his knee and he begins to cry
His father lifts him up and whispers in his ear
What a comfort to have his father oh, so near

And I know when I'm alone
You are there in my heart
That's the gift you've given me

We run so hard so fast like horses on the range
Far away are we from the narrow gate
Look around in fear, only see the open plain
I feel your hand upon my shoulder; you're never far away

And I know when I'm alone
You are there in my heart
That's the gift you've given me

A little boy goes running by
His father picks him up and raises him on high
Running so fast so hard against the raging tide
Wandering as we do we're never far out of sight

And I know when I'm alone
You are there in my heart
That's the gift you've given me

The gift you've given me …

The gift you've given me …

I Will See You

Words and music: Benjamin K. Bachman Copyright 2008
Produced by Larry B. Bachman
Vocals: Hale Baskin
Keyboards: Andrew Frye
Strings: Milo Deering
Percussion: Eric Morgan

Someday, someday I will see you.
Walking in that paradise we planned so long ago,
And my road leads so far from home.

Today the sun reminded me that I'm not alone;
Because somewhere it's shining from the moon through your window.
And in my head I can see your face, and I can feel that you're near me.
I know that if I can reach the sun I can wipe away your tears.

But if the fire of the sun begins to try and turn me away.
I'll use the memory of your love to guide me,
But my road leads far from home.

So tell me . . . tell me all your secrets . . .
I'll put them in a box of flowers I will keep them near me.
I will give you my heart with a picture so you won't forget me . . . don't forget me.
We'll embrace each other, say hello or maybe to say good bye.

The rivers calling me, the wind is telling me the time has come again.
My love for you is real, the pain it doesn't heal, we know it's not the end
. . .
But my road leads far from home.

Tell me . . . tell me all your secrets . . .
I'll put them in a box of flowers I will keep them near me.

The rivers calling me, the wind is telling me the time has come again.
My love for you is real the pain it doesn't heal we know it's not the end.
But my road leads far from home . . . but my road leads far from home.

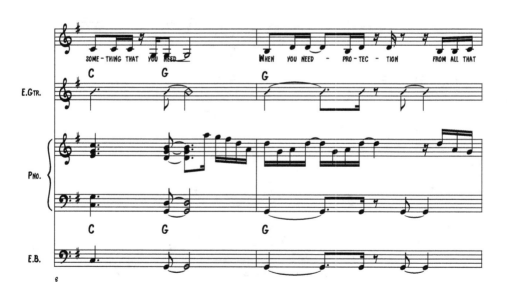

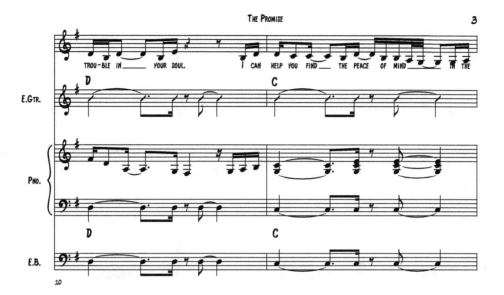

The Promise

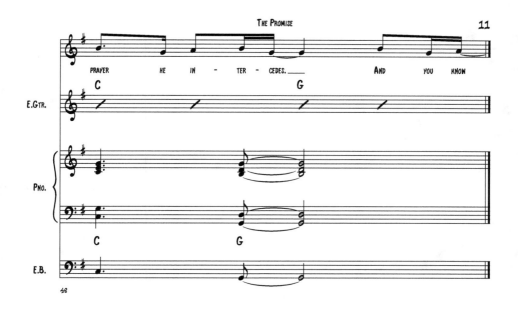

CHORUS/INTRO/OUT...

IN MEMORY OF SCOTT BACHMAN
06/24/56-10/18/22

I have been humbled by my brother Scott's bravery. So I have dedicated this book first, to my Lord and Savior Jesus Christ, who has brought us thus far. And second, to my brother, Scott, who at this writing was in the midst of a battle for his life. Prayer was continual for his rebound from the terrible disease of cancer, which was multiplied by other extensive health issues.

Scott Eugene Bachman, 66, slipped quietly into eternal rest on October 18, 2022, with his wife Brenda and brother Larry and sister-in-law Claudia by his side.

During the past few months, my brother and I got to spend some quality time reuniting; it enabled us to reminisce about days gone by. Scott has done much throughout the years, musically, for people in his local community. He gave lessons. He gave people a leg up through a venue that allowed vocalists and musicians to participate in open-mic events. Individuals who, if not for Scott, would never have gotten a chance to perform. One such person sent a letter to Scott. They told him how much they valued and enjoyed the open-mic opportunities. That it gave them purpose and brought them out from a dark place.

These are the kinds of things that none of us know about when we put forth the effort of kindness and opportunity. This is Scott's legacy; he had concern for others and gave them hope, and he was very kind in opening a local venue where musicians could share their craft.

Merged into this book's story line is Scott's playing lead guitar, and the band he played with called The Trainwreck Survivors, which included

John Erdley on drums, Geoff Craven on keys and strings, Bruce Bozyk on bass, and Brian Noaker on various instruments.

Scott played guitar, electric and acoustic, on the recording of "The Promise," the song this story is about. In the YouTube video it is sung by Shana Saint (https://1ref.us/23k).

Scott loved music and he loved playing his guitar. He taught himself how to play when he was eighteen. He used to tell Brenda that he had a jukebox constantly playing in his head! In the late sixties, I introduced him to the music scene, and it wasn't long before he was playing in a band and traveling throughout the region doing what he loved. He had the privilege of recording at the Record Plant in New York City, at Patrick McGuire Recording in Arlington, Texas, and locally, with his band members in a band called PA Crude.

He mentored younger musicians and always hoped he had changed their lives for the better. For fellow musicians and family members alike, it is a loss of a brother, a comrade, and friend, but most important, Brenda has lost all of the above, as well as a loving and caring husband.

Scott spent the majority of his life as a full-time musician and teacher. In the past he worked at the Middleburg Golf Club, Listening Booth, and Wall to Wall Sound and Video. He worked in construction and did painting, and most recently, worked at the Rusty Rail Brewing Company and Three Beards Brewery.

Scott also loved being on the Susquehanna River in the summer on his pontoon with Brenda and friends. He enjoyed gardening, spending time in the outdoors, and socializing around a campfire.

AN OLD MAN'S LAMENT
LARRY B. BACHMAN 07/12/18

(For my father: Because it was the last question I ever asked him.)

"Time," he said, "carries all regret;
The winter of life harbors my discontent.
My hands now gnarled and peculiar,
I stare at my reflection, it holds no future."

Content by the fires warmth, outside the snow falls
Unfamiliar shadows danced through hallowed halls.
Agitated he cried, "Legacy ... nothing here at all?
None worthy ... not one left to call!"

A silent pause, the ticking of the clock ...
A hand moves in time, and whispers, "Tic toc ... tic toc,"

"It's not right that they should go before I!
I've outlived most of my children and my wife!"

The old man watched as children played outside.
He drew a breath, paused, and breathed a labored sigh.
"You know I chased dreams that mattered to only I.
That being my greatest sin, perhaps my greatest lie!"

"There ... in the children our spirit lives on my friend.
The torch must be passed or will never be again."
Frost gave way to places on the window that he touched.
Ice crystals quickly repainted with winter's brush.

A silent pause ... the ticking of the clock . . .
A hand moves in time, and whispers, "Tic toc ... tic toc."

"It's just not right, and to me so unfair.
Friends are all gone, God seems to have left me here?"

"Ah, I can hear the music once again," He said,
A song long lost within," he tapped upon his head.
He smiled and moved his hands in time.
His eyes, they sparkled as he sang a familiar rhyme.

I tried to listen now ... I tried to understand.
Standing on the outsed ... I could not comprehend.
Far within in himself ... somewhere on a brighter day,
In a place ... in a time ... with God on holiday.

A silent pause ... the ticking of the clock . . .
A hand moves in time, and whispers, "Tic toc ... tic toc!"

"Sir," I asked him plainly, "Do you know just who I am?"
He looked concerned and answered, "Of course I do, you are my son."

The Trainwreck Survivors
Scott Bachman, Geof Craven, Bruce Bosnik and John Erdley

Scott Bachman

Geof Craven and John Erdley

Shana Saint

Milo Deering

Eric Sipe

Hale Baskin

Arron Delosantos

Scott Bachman and Benjamin Bachman

*Joey the engineer extraordinaire,
Scott Bachman and Larry Bachman*

Eric Morgan

TEACH Services, Inc.
PUBLISHING

We invite you to view the complete
selection of titles we publish at:
www.TEACHServices.com

We encourage you to write us
with your thoughts about this,
or any other book we publish at:
info@TEACHServices.com

TEACH Services' titles may be purchased in
bulk quantities for educational, fund-raising,
business, or promotional use.
bulksales@TEACHServices.com

Finally, if you are interested in seeing
your own book in print, please contact us at:
publishing@TEACHServices.com
We are happy to review your manuscript at no charge.